# Pintsized Pioneers

## Taming the Frontier, One Chore at a Time

Preston Lewis
and
Harriet Kocher Lewis

San Angelo, Texas

ISBN: 978-1-964830-04-9
Imprint: Bariso Press

Edited by: Harriet Kocher Lewis
Cover design by: Preston Lewis

Library of Congress Control Number: 2024912676

Book One of the Pintsized Pioneers Series

Cover Illustration: DALL-E
Printed in the United States of America

With Thanks To

**Scott and Melissa**

For All the Chores
They Handled for Us
As They Grew Up

**Bariso Press**

Harriet Kocher Lewis
Editor and Publisher

# CONTENTS

# Introduction

Children tread lightly through the pages of Old West history.

Often overlooked, if not completely ignored in accounts of frontier life, Old West children not only frolicked like kids everywhere, but they also played a critical role in taming the West through their labor. Even at early ages, they handled chores that freed their parents to take on more arduous tasks or to accept jobs for wages that helped frontier families make ends meet.

Sometimes a family's survival depended upon the youngest members handling tasks at ages as young as three. Their unheralded contributions to the Old West remain an obscure aspect of pioneer history.

Though they may have been called yearlings, sprouts, tendsomes, moppets, kids, younglings, young 'uns and tadpoles, those diminutive nicknames belie the asset that children became on the farms, on the ranches and in towns out west.

In 1850 Americans under the age of sixteen made up approximately forty-five percent of the country's growing population. By 1950 that percentage had declined to just over twenty-seven percent of the total populace.

One reason frontier children's roles remain obscure is few youngsters left contemporary accounts of their lives. More often than not, narratives of adolescent frontier life came decades later by old-timers recalling their early years in the Old West. As wonderful as those recollections are of pioneer childhoods, they lack the adolescent innocence of stories written before the children reached maturity. Consequently, this story is told not so much through the eyes of children when they were young, but through the bespectacled eyes of the elderly looking back upon their formative years.

*Pintsized Pioneers: Taming the Frontier, One Chore at a Time* spotlights children on the frontier and how their chores contributed to the success of their elders and to the settling of the Old West. This book is written for today's youth and focuses on frontier youngsters from birth to age sixteen. Using accounts mostly put to paper decades after the experience of the childhood pioneers, the authors concentrate on the frontier as lived by Anglo settlers, instead of the Native American and Hispanic populations that often preceded them.

Today we take for granted the technology that has made our lives so convenient. If you imagine a life without electricity, you begin to understand how difficult living on the frontier must have been. By the late nineteenth-century, American cities began to provide electricity as they approached the twentieth century, but small towns and rural Americans everywhere were less fortunate. On into the Great Depression in the 1930s, many citizens, particularly on rural farms in the South and on ranches in the West, lacked the convenience of electricity and its labor-saving benefits.

Communication in most areas of the frontier traveled no faster than a horse could run. While the telegraph connected many towns, and primitive telephones later provided simple but costly connections for the wealthy, average Americans relied on word-of-mouth and newspapers for their understanding of national and world affairs. Moreover, they depended on handwritten letters to stay in touch with family and friends back east or wherever they lived.

Life then was much slower than the pace of the twenty-first century, and it was much closer to the source of sustenance. Today the supermarket just down the street provides foods from around the world. In the nineteenth century, however, food was more likely to come from the family garden in the summer and fall and from the foodstuffs the family canned, preserved, and stored for the winter and spring. Families raised or hunted their meat. Pioneers lived a very elemental existence with considerable time and effort spent on feeding, clothing, and housing themselves. With no social safety net, frontier folks relied on each other to succeed. Fathers and mothers carried substantial workloads, but even their youngest children contributed in small ways with their little hands and bodies.

Wherever possible, the authors of *Pintsized Pioneers* have illustrated the role of children through anecdotes of those who grew up in the West. Most of these stories come from history books, diaries, newspaper articles, or recollections of those who matured on the frontier. One elegant source on the childhood frontier was *Boy Life on the Prairie* by Hamlin Garland. Though he fictionalizes the names in the 1899 account, Garland later admitted the book was autobiographical. Thus, whenever *Boy Life on the Prairie* is quoted, it is done with Garland's name rather than that of his fictional counterpart Lincoln Stewart. Otherwise, all names—if they were available—are those of the children or their family members. While Garland was a published author familiar with good grammar and syntax, not all those quoted in the following pages were as well educated. In direct quotes, their words are left as they were recorded, even if they included grammatical errors.

While similarities existed in their lives, the frontier experiences of youngsters varied from place to place because the West differed from the rest of the country. Once west of the Mississippi River, especially beginning at the $98^{th}$ meridian, rainfall and timber diminished. Without consistent rain and adequate wood for construction, westerners and their children—unlike their eastern counterparts—faced special challenges in building successful homes and lives.

Additionally, work on a farm differed from that on a ranch. Tasks in town varied, depending on if the community was a mining enclave or a railroad stop. Further, life on the Great Plains contrasted significantly from the experience in the Pacific Northwest, where rain and timber were more in line with that enjoyed east of the Mississippi River. Varying weather from location to location also created different duties for little ones and their parents.

To address these variances in an organized fashion, the authors have divided this account into chapters with differing themes. The first chapter deals with the allure of the West and the tasks of children making the trek west, especially on the Oregon Trail. Chapter Two addresses the universal need and search for fire and water. In the third chapter, the writers address children's contributions to feeding their families. For the fourth chapter, the authors examine housekeeping on the frontier.

Chapter Five explores farming and the difficulties of raising a crop and livestock in a challenging environment. Ranching is the focus of the sixth chapter since the cattle industry is such an important part of the Old West in both fact and fiction. The seventh chapter examines town children and how they helped their parents. Chapter Eight looks at the challenges of making ends meet on the frontier. The ninth and concluding chapter offers lessons on what we can learn from the pioneering experience of yearlings, sprouts, tendsomes, moppets, kids, younglings, and tadpoles.

In the end, the authors hope *Pintsized Pioneers: Taming the Frontier, One Chore at a Time* gives the young 'uns of a bygone era their due for helping settle the West. In their stories reside lessons for today's youth about the value of work and how it can help them in their lives and in their futures.

# Pintsized Pioneers

Chapter One

# Getting There

The allure of the West attracted nineteenth-century Americans like magnets drew metal shards. The pioneers sought a better life, even if it meant starting over from scratch. They searched for their own slice of heaven on earth. Some found it. Many did not.

Thirteen-year-old Mormon pioneer Ruth May discovered it in 1867 when she reached her destination, Salt Lake City. "The sky was blue and radiant, the valley fair, and the grand old mountains proudly guarded the home of the prophets. The family took a bath in a washbasin, put on our best clothes, and went to the tabernacle services. My dreams came true, and all was well in Zion."

For other children, their destination fell short of paradise. Years after young Ruth reached Salt Lake City, seven-year-old Grace Snyder eyed the desolate barrenness of her new home in Custer County, Nebraska. "I can still see the homestead as it looked when we pulled into it that day—just two naked little soddies squatting on a bare, windswept ridge above a narrow, winding canyon."

Pioneer children were swept across the West, wherever their folks took them. Some parents desired land, while others pursued riches. Many wanted a new start where they could determine their own future or escape an embarrassing past elsewhere. Some craved adventure while a number sought freedom from the shackles of social or religious constraints back east.

To fulfill those ambitions, pioneer men and women had to "get there" wherever "there" was. In the early days of the transcontinental migration, California and Oregon Territory were "there." Later, the destinations changed to Texas to grow cotton; to the Great Plains where farmland was available for homesteading; to Utah, where Mormons found their own Zion; or to the next county over, as long as it was closer to the setting sun.

Horace Greeley, himself an easterner and founder/editor of the *New York Tribune*, articulated the spirit of the times in an 1865 *Tribun*e editorial. In one of the most famous quotations in American history, Greeley wrote, "Go West, young man, and grow up with the country!"

One emigrant father, William Rudd, echoed Greeley's comment, explaining he took his family west "to get a new start and let [my] children grow up with the country."

During the early decades of the nineteenth century, men especially looked to the West, some taking their wives and children into the wilderness. In the wake of the Civil War, even more people headed toward the setting sun for a myriad of reasons. Wherever men traveled westward with their families, their offspring worked beside them, handling tasks and chores along the trail. The older the child, the harder the jobs and the greater the responsibilities they assumed. However large or small their contributions to the family's well-being, their help freed their parents from those duties and allowed them to navigate the treacherous trails and unforeseen challenges ahead.

On the way west, families could ill afford idle children. Along the trail, adolescents had to pull and push their own weight as John Stucki later remembered of his 1850 trip. "I have never forgotten how when I, a nine-year-old boy, would be so tired that I would wish I could sit down for just a few minutes. How much good it would do to me. But instead of that, my dear, nearly worn-out father would ask me if I could not push a little more on the handcart."

For five years starting in 1856, Latter-Day Saints pioneers used two-wheeled handcarts about the size of a city peddler's cart on the Mormon Trail. Ten handcart expeditions headed for Zion during that period, with the men pulling the carts and the women and children pushing them when necessary. Without draft animals to care for, the handcarts provided more time each day to travel. Loaded with supplies and a few personal belongings for four or five people, the carts advanced on the muscle power of the emigrants. For every twenty carts, a regular wagon was assigned to carry the family's heavier possessions.

After the 1804-1806 Lewis and Clark Expedition proved the Pacific Ocean was accessible by land, a variety of trails opened to exploit the Corps of Discovery's findings. The Oregon Trail became the most significant, extending more than 2,100 miles from the Missouri River to the Willamette Valley in Oregon Territory. The trail crossed portions of the future states of Kansas, Nebraska, Wyoming, Idaho, and Oregon. Originally established by fur traders beginning in 1811, the Oregon Trail in 1836 handled its first westbound migrant train.

The eastern half of the Oregon Trail and its parallel routes provided the starting point for travelers going to northern California on the California Trail, originating in 1843; to Utah on the Mormon Trail, beginning in 1847; and to Montana gold rush country on the Bozeman Trail, commencing in 1863.

The Gila Trail, variously known as the Southern Emigrant Trail or the Butterfield Trail, provided a route for travelers destined for southern California. Various other trails through Texas and New Mexico Territory fed into the Gila Trail, which crossed Arizona into California at Yuma.

Between 1841, when the first emigrant child reached California, and 1865, when the Civil War ended, some 40,000 children moved west from the Missouri and Mississippi rivers toward the Pacific Coast. Even more followed after the War Between the States, many settling on the plains in the country's midsection to take advantage of the Homestead Act of 1862.

At three years of age, Sarah Sophia Moulding was among the young girls who made the sojourn with her family. "As little as I was, I can remember the noise of the wagon and the jingle-jangle of the pots and kettles fastened underneath and at the sides of the wagon. I remember the dust and dirt from the wagons in front of us."

Then nine-year-old Agnes Caldwell had other memories of the journey. "Although only tender years of age, I can yet close my eyes and see everything in panoramic precision before me—the ceaseless walking, walking, ever to remain in my memory."

In 1850, the year after gold was discovered at Sutter's Mill in California, records at Wyoming's Fort Laramie documented ninety-nine children, a hundred and nineteen women and 17,443 men passed through that stop on the Oregon Trail. Once the gold fever died down, greater percentages of women and children accompanied the men on their westward trek.

The journey west on the Oregon Trail and its many branches often began at St. Joseph, Missouri, where in 1849 fourteen-year-old Sallie Hester observed, "As far as the eye can reach, so great is the emigration, you see nothing but wagons … a vast army on wheels—crowds of men, women, and lots of children."

One fourteen-year-old boy recalled the start of the trip "as a great picnic excursion." Periodically along the way, youngsters saw jaw-dropping natural wonders. Upon seeing Devil's Gate Canyon in southwest Wyoming, eleven-year-old Willie Ward in the words of his mother "expressed astonishment and awe mingled with fear, but after looking awhile he became perfectly enraptured. He laughed and sang and appeared as if he hardly knew how to express his delight."

By the midpoint of his journey to Oregon, eight-year-old Jesse Applegate remembered "looking far away in the direction we were traveling across a dreary sage plain, to all appearances extending to the end of the earth.... To me, Oregon was a word without meaning."

Despite the excitement of starting a journey to Oregon and California or the thrill of seeing natural wonders, the tedium of trail life as described by young Jesse soon set in for children and adults alike. Whatever the trail and no matter the emigrants' destination, children's chores were similar. They gathered wood or buffalo dung for fires to cook their food and warm themselves. They looked after younger siblings. They toted water. They helped set up and take down camp. They watched after chickens and herded livestock. And, they stood night guard and defended camp from intruders. Save for infants and the youngest of children, most adolescents—unless they had ponies—walked along the trail, adding to their daily toil and exhaustion. Sometimes youngsters atop their mounts rode ahead of the wagons to look out for trail hazards or water.

Young Sarah Cummins was one of the lucky ones with a "riding nag" that she would mount each day and ride in advance of the caravan looking for difficult stretches of trail or exploring water crossings to make certain hidden boulders didn't obstruct the wagon path.

As their less fortunate peers afoot trod along the route, they had various tasks. "Gathering buffalo chips was Esther's and my job," recalled then eight-year-old Florence Weeks, who gathered the dung with her sister for fuel. "We were rather finicky about it at first, but found they were as dry as a chip of wood. We had a basket with a handle on each side to carry them."

When emigrant trains stopped for the night, kids had additional duties. The older youth helped unharness the horses or unyoke the oxen. Some kids released the chickens from their cages to look for bugs and worms. While the fowls sought their supper, the children collected eggs they might use for their own family's meal that night.

One of the most hated chores by youngsters on the trail or at home was churning butter because of its repetitive tedium. Twelve-year-old Catherine Adams of Illinois recalled how her father solved that problem on the journey. After the kids milked the cows in the morning, they strained the milk into churns, which their father loaded in the back of the wagons. "At night," she recalled, "through the constant motion of the wagon all day, there would be pieces of rich, yellow butter clinging to the sides of the churn; some of them would be the size of goose eggs."

When the pioneers camped near rivers or springs, teenager Maria Elliot loved to gather berries that grew along the watercourses, calling them the "richest wild fruit I ever saw." Near streams, children also drew buckets of water to meet the evening needs and to fill their water barrels to quench thirsts on down the trail.

Sometimes, though, the water was too salty or brackish for man or animal. “My, how we boys and girls worked day after day to keep our cows and sheep from drinking too large a dose at one time of this brackish water,” Susan Noble, fifteen, remembered of her 1847 journey. “The weather was so hot, though, and the animals increased in their thirst by the salty country … In spite of our poundings and pleadings, they would gorge themselves [on brackish water] … and then almost immediately begin being sick.”

On waterless stretches of trail, thirst plagued all. Nine-year-old Joseph Smith remembered one such day as he advanced beside Thom, his favorite ox, which he had raised from a calf. “Many times while traveling sandy or rough roads, on long, thirsty drives, my oxen were lowing with the heat and fatigue. I would put my arms around Thom’s neck and cry bitter tears! That was all I could do.”

Even on waterless sections of the trail, the evening stop brought some relief. As the nightly camp was being established, young boys would head out with guns and fishing poles to see if they could bring additional and varied fare to the table because on travel days, dusk provided the most time and opportunity for a filling meal. Fourteen-year-old Rebecca Nutting welcomed the change from the standard meats of bacon and salt pork. “How we did relish the fish and venison and buffalo steaks,” she said.

Eleven-year-old Elisha Brooks described a typical travel day menu as “dried apples for breakfast, drink water for dinner, and [a] swell … supper.”

After meals there were dishes to clean, animals to bed down and night watches to man. Even at eleven, young Elisha and his brother stood regular guard over the camp and herd. One night the Brooks boys had just bedded down the livestock, "when suddenly an Indian yell rent the air, and wild, rushing, leaping shadows went hurtling by with shrieks and tumult awfully appealing. Our skeleton beasts sprang up and away like a whirlwind … until the sound died in the distance, and silence fell upon us again."

Indians remained a constant fear among trail travelers, and though attacks did happen, they only affected a minute number of families along the route. Even so, the occasional raids could be terrifying and deadly, like an 1858 assault in Apache lands on the Gila Trail. During a brief noon stop for lunch, young Sally Fox spied an approaching band of Indians. As she screamed, "The Indians are coming … to kill us," her mom gathered Sally and her siblings and shoved them into the back of their wagon. Sally's half-sister Kate recalled, "My mother wrapped us all round with feather-beds, blankets, and comforters" to protect the little ones from arrows and bullets, but too late for little Sally, who felt something warm running down her side. It turned out to be her own blood.

Kate recalled the moment Sally realized she had sustained an injury. "Looking down, she saw an arrow which had pierced her flesh and protruded its flinty head from the wound. 'Mother,' she cried, 'I am shot' and fainted. My mother drew the arrow backward through the wound." Sally was one of a dozen wounded in the attack, but she would survive. Two others, including her stepfather, would not, dying in defense of the wagon train. Sally survived to live a long life and saved the bloodstained garment for the rest of her life, never mending the ragged arrow holes in her dress.

Despite Sally's girlhood experience, the danger of an Indian attack on most emigrant caravans was slim. By contrast, Indian thefts, night raids of livestock, and demands for tribute to cross their lands were more common than physical assaults on pioneers.

In 1861 then teenager George Humpherys recalled one encounter when a large band of Indians threatened to attack his wagon train unless they received ten yokes of oxen, a thousand pounds of flour, three hundred pounds of sugar, a hundred pounds of coffee, and a hundred pounds of bacon. Realizing negotiations were fruitless, the wagon master asked the chief to accompany him to a nearby wagon to get the approval of the real leader of the caravan. The "real leader" turned out to be a traveler stricken with smallpox. When the afflicted man arose in the back of the wagon at the wagon master's call, the Indians saw his blistered and scabbed face. The chief shouted, "Smallpox!"

As Humphreys recalled, the intruders turned their horses about and raced away. "We could not get sight of an Indian for three weeks after that. We had to conclude," Humphreys noted with tongue in cheek, "that the smallpox was a very good thing to have close by."

Even though the risk of death was minimal from the indigenous people, the fear of Indians was powerful enough to scare off the teamster Elisha Brooks' mother had hired to lead her family from Michigan to California to join her husband. The teamster deserted the family after "the air was thick with tales of Indian massacres, starvation, and pestilence." Once he abandoned the family, young Elisha Brooks and his brothers, ages four to thirteen, became the "men" of her wagon and handled most of the chores normally attended by adult males.

Though Indians concerned many travelers, accidents and illnesses constituted a bigger threat. Diseases like cholera, dysentery, and other maladies endangered pioneer families even more. The farther an immigrant train advanced, the more often children had to pick up the duties of their parents because of injury, illness, or death. No chore on the trail was more dreaded than digging a grave, a task handled by men and maturing boys like John Breen, then fourteen. Adults and youngsters alike pitched in to gather rocks to cover graves so wild animals would not dig up the corpses. "Death had become so common an event," observed young Breen, "that it was looked upon as a matter of course."

Eight-year-old Florence Weeks on an 1859 wagon train to California confided in her diary, "One had the oddest felling seeing those graves in such lonely places, but it made no difference to the ones who was gone. It was the thought of going on without them."

Trail children lost friends, siblings and sometimes—most unsettling of all—their parents. On the Mormon Trail eight-year-old Laura Swenson saw her father die in a wagon accident and a week later witnessed her mother's passing during childbirth, leaving her and her four younger sisters orphans.

Pioneer John H. Clark made a June 30, 1852, diary entry of overtaking a "little girl, who had lingered far behind" her wagon train. She was bawling and her feet were bleeding from the sharp flint stone on the road. He dismounted and took her into his arms, asking if she was crying because of her injured feet. "No," she sobbed, "nothing hurts me now. They buried my father and mother yesterday. I don't want to live any longer. They took me away from my sweet mother and put her in the ground."

The frequency of death on the trail hardened some children to its implications. Scottish born Peter Howard McBride, at age six, lost his father, also on the Mormon Trail. After the elder McBride was buried, young Peter realized what had happened and rushed to the grave, bawling. With efforts to console him failing, Peter blurted out amongst the tears, "My father had my fish hooks in his pocket, and I want them." He was hardened enough to death to subordinate the loss of his father to the value of those fish hooks on down the road to provide nourishment and help him and his siblings survive.

Fanny Fry had the unsettling experience of seeing her own grave. While pushing a handcart on the Mormon Trail, she fell in front of the cart, and the wheel ran over her. Knocked unconscious and seemingly lifeless, Fanny appeared dead to all around her. She was not. When Fanny came to, she found herself half sewn into the blanket that would have been her burial shroud. Wiggling from the cloth and standing to prove her vitality, Fanny realized the two-foot-deep hole the men had been digging nearby was for her.

Certainly, death on the trail resulted in a significant loss to a family, but sickness created a burden, pulling another person or two from their daily routines. Often it fell to teenage girls to tend to the ailing. Besides losing his father and his fish hooks, Peter McBride remembered his mother being sick on most of the journey to Utah. In addition to caring for her, Peter recalled "my [older] sister Jenetta had the worry of us children. She carried water from the river to do the cooking. Her shoes gave out, and she walked through the snow barefoot, actually leaving bloody tracks in the snow."

Every trip across the country to the Pacific Coast or even to Utah was a race against time. Wherever it began, the journey had to wait until the land had hardened enough after the seasonal thaw to support heavily loaded wagons. Departure also had to await emerging spring grass in quantities adequate to provide grazing for the animals. Once the venture started, especially on the northern trails, the pioneer caravan needed to reach its destination before the winter snows blanketed any mountain ranges they must cross.

Consequently, every day on the expedition had to start early to maximize the daylight hours and the distance traveled. Even before darkness began to evaporate each morning, children and adults arose to start another tedious daily routine. Before dawn they were harnessing livestock, taking down tents, packing the wagons, eating a quick breakfast and hitting the trail to take advantage of the morning cool or as much sunshine as possible.

If pioneer caravans on the Oregon, California, and Mormon trails got too tardy a start or tarried along the way, they risked being stranded in blizzards or snowbound in the mountain ranges they had to cross. On the southern routes, water became scarcer in the fall, making late desert crossings equally dangerous.

Whichever trail the pioneers took, each had its own set of challenges and dangers. Eleven-year-old Hermann Scharmann and his fifteen-year-old brother Jacob helped their father shepherd their mother and two-and-a-half year old sister across the country. But the situation turned grim as they crossed a stretch of desert nearing California. They grew worried their team would not survive. They had good reason to fret as the brothers with their father counted 1,663 dead or dying oxen and eighty-one "shattered or abandoned wagons" left behind by the men without families who had proceeded afoot.

As their prospects for survival diminished, young Herman recognized it and told his dad, "If you and I were alone, we would do as the other travelers did, take our knapsacks on our backs and go on foot." When things turned desperate, Herman's father left the boys to take care of their mother and sister while he set out on foot for supplies. The boys protected their mother, but buried their sister, who starved to death. When their father returned within the week with the provisions that saved them, the brothers tearfully informed him their sister had died.

In another account of traveling hardships, eleven-year-old Henry Ferguson and his seven siblings left Jasper County, Iowa, in the spring of 1849, headed to California with their gold-seeking father. As they neared their destination late in the travel season, trouble befell their party in the mountains after a tree toppled, killing four in an accompanying family, and injuring four of Henry's younger siblings. Desperate to get the injured ones to a settlement and medical attention but not wanting to abandon his belongings, Henry's father left him and his thirteen-year-old brother John behind. He took the rest of the family in an empty wagon to seek help, promising Henry and John he would return in two weeks.

Of the scary responsibility, Henry wrote, "Our living was very scant, having really nothing to eat except for what we could kill with our guns." They feared starving—or worse, becoming a meal for grizzly bears, whose tracks they found around the wagon each morning—yet they had to live up to their promise of protecting the family belongings. For meals, they ate a half-pound of dried peaches they discovered hidden in the wagon, woodpeckers, and a small deer John shot a mile from the wagon. Some of the food made them violently sick, "throwing up all that was in them and suffering terribly," as Henry described it.

Even so, they survived, enduring a terrible rain storm that delayed their father's return a couple of days. When he did arrive, he brought his oldest boys some bread, but the trail was too saturated to drive the heavily loaded wagon. So, he left them behind again until he could return with additional teams. "We stayed and watched the wagons which contained all our earthly belongings, until at the end of another long week, father came again, bringing plenty of teams to take our wagons to the settlement which was only twenty-five miles away."

No matter where each journey began or where it ended, it took its toll on people, animals, and wagons. Upon reaching her destination of Vernon, California, after an overland trip, fourteen-year-old Sallie Hester wrote in her diary, "Well, after five months' trip from St. Joe, Missouri, our party of fifty wagons, now only thirteen, has at last reached this haven of rest. Strangers in a strange land—what will the future be?"

That was the question asked by most who survived the overland journey by the end of the Civil War and those who later traveled to the Great Plains to claim homesteads after 1865 and Appomattox. Other families kept looking for a prosperous future by moving to an adjacent county or from one state to another.

Five-year-old Lillian "Lily" Klasner was one of those, moving with her family from central Texas to New Mexico Territory in late 1866. Though the Klasner family traveled about five hundred miles, roughly a quarter of the distance of the overland caravans, the challenges were comparable, passing through woodless and waterless stretches that tried man and beast. The family herded some three hundred cattle, two hundred sheep and dozens of horses.

Lily remembered, "The oxen (teams) traveled at about the same pace as that of the slowly moving herd and that gave us time to keep the 'possum-belly filled. This was a big dry hide for carrying fuel. When we saw a dry stick or cow chip, we ran, picked it up, and threw it into the possum-belly swung beneath the wagon so that when we camped dry fuel would be available."

When they began the trip, wood provided their kindling, but the farther west they traveled, the scarcer it became, forcing them to dig up the roots from mesquite bushes. "The roots make excellent wood," she remembered, "though they are usually covered with soil. Mesquite makes a fine, hot fire, but smokes cooking utensils badly so that cleaning them is almost impossible.... When mesquite was not available, buffalo chips made a quick, hot fire but [large] quantities were required for cooking. Sometimes we had to depend upon bear grass, which produces more blaze than heat."

The 'possum-belly also carried newborn calves and lambs too weak to keep up with their mothers. "Sometimes one had to be carried two or three days before it was strong enough to follow its mammy," Lily recalled. "If one (a calf) gave out, a man picked it up and carried it on his horse to the wagon for another ride in the 'possum-belly. There was a similar problem with the sheep, which Mother had refused to leave behind. She had raised this small flock from dogie lambs given her by neighboring ranchers. They had learned to come at her call of "Lamby, Lamby" for food or salt. She had sheared them, carded the wool, spun it into thread or yarn, woven cloth for clothing and blankets, and knitted our stockings. No wonder she thought them indispensable."

The Klasner family made it to New Mexico Territory safely, just one of hundreds of families on the move, trying to secure their future on the lands west of the Mississippi.

Most folks on the trail ultimately reached their destination, though not always without the loss of family members or some of their worldly goods. Seventeen-year-old Margaret Judd summed up her trip across the country. "Our journey was like all such journeys—it had its pleasant side, and its unpleasant side. When the sun was shining and the roads were good, we trotted along feeling that we would soon be at our destination, but when the rain poured down and the roads were so bad that we could not travel—then that was the other side."

But on good days and bad, the chores remained for man, woman, and child, as shown in Margaret McNeil's recollection of her toilsome trek cross country at age thirteen. "I walked every step of the way across the plains and drove a cow; and a large part of that way, I carried my brother on my back."

Ten-year-old Francis Marion Watkins left Albia, Iowa, on April 1, 1865, bound for Petaluma, California, with his parents, five brothers, sister, niece, and nephew. Four and a half months later, they reached their destination, averaging just over thirteen miles a day on the trip. After four years in California, the family in 1869 decided to take up homesteading in Kansas instead. Thanks to the Transcontinental Railroad, they made the return trip in days, averaging around 245 miles a day on the train. Watkins, by then fourteen years old, noted, “Everything was changed.”

Young Watkins was correct. Mechanization and industrialization would continue to transform transportation and work life in the decades to come, but not in time to diminish the chores handled by boys and girls on the trail once they reached their parents’ destinations.

Chapter Two

# Fire and Water

Rather than a Garden of Eden, many youngsters traveling west, particularly to the Great Plains, soon realized their new home was more a "garden of needin'!" They were always needing water and combustibles for fire.

Though the journey for the boys and girls may have ended once they reached their destinations, their chores continued. Just as on the trail, no tasks were more important than providing fire and water, a task often assigned to the children.

Born in central Texas before moving to southeastern New Mexico Territory at the age of five, Lily Klasner later recalled those hardscrabble years. "Though the pioneers had their faults and weaknesses, few could shirk work or indulge in idleness. In a very literal sense, work was a life preserver and every member of a family had his tasks."

Then, as now, water was the foremost necessity for life, whether human, animal, or plant. Likewise, combustibles were required to fuel the fires for cooking food year round and for heating their homes in the fall and winter. Pioneer children toted water for family and livestock. They also gathered wood where they found it. Where wood was scarce, they collected animal dung and yellowed plants that would burn. The older the youngsters grew and the stronger they became, the heavier the loads of water and fuel they carried.

In the early decades of the westward migration, the "overlanders," as they were called, left timbered and watered regions east of the Mississippi River for land similarly blessed with streams and forests in Oregon Territory and California. Later pioneers who settled the Great Plains extending from the Canadian border south into west Texas found fewer watercourses and even less timber.

Consequently, many prairie families had to travel miles for water and even farther for wood, relying instead on buffalo and cattle dung to fuel their fireplaces or stoves. Supplying water and fuel was difficult enough everywhere on the frontier, but it was downright dangerous when pioneers encroached on lands where Indians still roamed.

While living in Texas, young Lily Klasner remembered how the menace of Comanche and Kiowa influenced the work schedule and the dress of her mother and older sister, even when Lily's father was present. "Mother and Sarah wore dresses during the day, but at dusk would change into men's clothes so a lurker might think there were three men in the house. They did all the milking, feeding, and bringing in wood and water well before dark, then bolted the doors and windows and did not open them until morning. No lights were used and, except in cold weather, no fires were built—people went to bed early and arose before daylight."

Even without the threat of Indians in daytime or darkness, toting water was a cumbersome chore for children, but water was essential for family drinking, cooking, and cleaning.

After she moved to New Mexico Territory, young Lily carried water from irrigation ditches the Hispanics called "acequias" to her new home. "During spring and summer irrigation, water for domestic use was taken from the acequias, one of which was close to the house. In the fall and winter when the ditches were empty, water had to be carried from the stream." After seeing Hispanic women haul water in earthen jugs called "ollas" on their heads, little Lily tried to imitate them. "I practiced attempting to stand with a small jar of water on my head, but never mastered the art." Instead, Lily toted her water in pails and watched in amazement the Hispanic women who could balance an olla on their heads and carry two pails of water as well.

Beyond the family requirement, their livestock also needed water to survive. Those pioneers fortunate enough to live near a stream could drive their animals to the creek to quench their thirsts. Where water courses were inaccessible, settlers had to deliver water to the animals.

That was a major undertaking. A thousand-pound bovine, for instance, required about ten gallons of water a day when the temperature stood at seventy degrees. A milk cow needed double that amount at the same temperature and, on average, produced a gallon of milk for every four and a half gallons of water it consumed. The hotter the weather, though, the more water the animals required.

With a gallon of water weighing eight pounds and five ounces, a milk cow on a mild day could consume more than a hundred and fifty pounds of water. Such amounts represented many a load for the children and their mothers, who were often responsible for distributing the precious liquid. Though the load was twice as heavy, children soon realized it was better to tote two water-filled pails than just one. A filled bucket in each hand was much easier to balance and resulted in less spillage. Some children opted to wear over their neck and shoulders a leather strap with a pail tied to each end to lighten the strain on their hands and arms.

Until a family could dig a well or afford to have one drilled, the farther they lived from a water source, the heavier the workload. Two western Kansas brothers, ages seven and twelve, hauled water from a creek five miles from their house to meet the need. They loaded empty barrels in the family wagon, then drove to the creek, and filled them a bucket full at a time before returning home with their precious commodity. The R.R. Singley family, who also settled in western Kansas, transported water for seven years until they dug a well.

A mother of three in California's Santa Clara Valley remembered on one "place we had no water, [and] had to go two miles to Campbell's Creek once a week. The men folks would take a large lumber wagon holding six barrels and go after the water." The children always helped.

Even if water was nearby or the home was blessed with a well, it didn't reduce the hassle of getting the liquid where it was needed. Prairie lass Matilda Peitzke remembered, "I often had to get water from a spring and carry it out to the field for drinking for the workers before I was old enough to do other field work." When Matilda aged sufficiently to handle more difficult chores, the responsibility of carrying water to workers fell on her younger siblings.

Because water was so difficult to find on the plains, pioneer families collected it wherever they could find it. After rains, water pooled in buffalo wallows, depressions in the ground where bison rolled around to shed dead hair and ticks. The liquid was dirty, but it was still water, and settlers used it for everything, including drinking once they had strained it through a cheese cloth.

Early pioneers fortunate enough to stake out their homestead near a stream or spring dug wells that could supply fresh water at twenty- or thirty-foot depths. Later arrivals settling on the vast prairies that made up the Great Plains had to dig more than a hundred feet to reach water. It was dangerous work for man and boy with the threat of cave-ins or of hitting gas pockets that could suffocate the diggers. The excavation was done with pick and shovel. The dirt and debris were pulled from the hole, a bucket at a time using the same windlass that had lowered the worker into the pit.

Rosetta Singley, daughter of the Kansas couple that hauled water to their place for seven years, recalled digging their family's first well, which reached a depth of a hundred and fifty feet. "It was a big job," fraught with danger, she said, but the reduced workload and the resulting fresh water were worth it.

Other families dug cisterns to capture and store rainwater for later use. Cisterns were usually no more than forty feet deep and either plastered or lined with stone to provide a clean storage receptacle. Dakota Territory lad Percy Ebbutt, fourteen, helped dig and finish the walls of the cistern on his folks' place. Periodically, he was lowered into the hole to clean it. Other pioneers hoarded empty tin cans to provide makeshift gutters that could drain water from a roof into a cistern. Some used flattened tin cans to make primitive shingles to roof their house and funnel runoff to a cistern. This had the added benefit of reducing leakage into the house during thunderstorms.

Even with a cistern or well on the homestead, children still had to work to produce the water, either dropping a bucket on a windlass into the hole or, if lucky, using a hand pump to lift the liquid from the ground. Settler Charles Schumacher of Stutsman County, North Dakota, required each of his four sons to deliver a hundred strokes of the pump handle each day to supply water for their kitchen. If they failed to meet their quota, they faced a lashing from their no-nonsense father's buggy whip.

From his Iowa boyhood Hamlin Garland remembered a typical morning before going to school. "After breakfast, all the cattle were turned into the yard and watered at the well. This meant a half-an-hour of hard pumping, but ended the morning duties."

In those days, "homework" came as much at the house as it did from school.

Just as essential as the search for water was the quest for wood and other combustibles to produce the fire to cook their food, to warm their homes and to heat water to launder their clothes. Finding fuel remained a challenge on the treeless prairies. Thankfully, the millions of buffalo that had roamed the region for centuries had left combustible calling cards in their wake. Buffalo dung would burn hot, but quick. So, large quantities were required, and a conical pile of buffalo chips stacked head high became a standard feature around sod houses on the Great Plains. Just as common inside the dwelling was a wooden box filled with buffalo patties next to the stove for ready access during cooking.

Women and children gathered the dung clods, collecting them in gunnysacks, baskets and even aprons. When traveling or walking across the prairie, children made a game of collecting the dried dung, a sort of "I Spy" to see who spotted the most. Pintsized pioneer Jesse Applegate turned the chore of finding prairie patties into a contest with his friends. Nine-year-old Illinois native Henry Brown amassed enough buffalo badges one day that he assigned his seven-year-old sister Mary Jane to guard his treasure.

When the trail drive era started after the Civil War, some homesteaders invited cowboys to bed their cattle down overnight on their unplowed land. Come the next morning, the settler's land was dotted with several hundred pounds of cow manure, which provided fuel or fertilizer for the spring crop, once the boys and girls gathered the “prairie coal.”

Other euphemisms for animal dung included “cow wood,” “prairie peat,” “meadow muffins,” “cow patties,” “cow chips,” “pancakes,” “surface coal,” “prairie plates,” “round browns,” and “prairie pancakes.” One young Texas Panhandle “chipper,” as those who gathered the dried droppings were sometimes called, filled his tow sack with dung and compared the chore “to picking cotton.” One pioneer mother claimed “chips were burned because they were cheap, quick and easy to gather, and could be collected by children who could not cut wood” or do other chores. For some chippers, though, the task grew wearisome as demonstrated by six-year-old Texan George Humphrey. Tired of retrieving surface coal to heat his mother’s wash pot, young George ran away from home to live with a neighboring family, at least temporarily.

In the Texas Panhandle, where wood was especially scarce, many children attending one-room schools gathered cow patties on the way to class to heat the school stove on cold winter days, adding another dimension to the concept of “school work.” In Deaf Smith County, Texas, boys and girls regularly took part in all-day “chip pickings” to provide fuel for the classroom heater.

The youthful Charley O’Kieffe remembered his “first chip harvest” as a family affair. The younger siblings “had to cover as much ground as possible, gathering up all the chips we could find and loading them in piles.” Then the older brothers filled the wagon for the ride home. At first, children and even some adults, particularly women, remained squeamish at handling the prairie brownies. With time, however, their fussiness evaporated because of necessity and familiarity. One Kansas grassland lass remembered her mother at first only retrieving dung patties with gloves. Within a short time, however, her mother was using her bare hands, even tossing patties into the stove and "going right on making biscuits without washing" her hands.

Young south plains resident W.E. Winn witnessed a similar sight at a ranch home he visited. "This woman would be making bread and have to put fuel in the stove. She would use her hands for the job and then give them a pat or two together and go right back to her bread making." Bothered by what he had witnessed, he could not eat the meal that evening. A traveling salesman invited to dine in the homes of customers witnessed a similar kitchen scene. After that, he vowed never to remain in the kitchen until the meal was on the table so he could enjoy the food without worrying about its preparation.

To extend the burning time of barnyard manure, some German immigrants mixed straw with cow manure and shaped the conglomerate into bricks they called "dung coal," a process they brought to America from their homeland.

But plentiful though prairie patties were, the animal dung did not last forever as the buffalo herds thinned and trail cattle became a threat to the cultivated acreage of the settlers. Consequently, pioneers turned to other fuels. In the frontier hierarchy of fuels wood remained the preferred source, though some woods burned better than others. Next came grubs or roots which were dug from the ground, a chore older boys often received. In the Southwest, mesquite roots were commonly dug and yanked from the earth. Though the mesquite root might be little more than an inch in diameter, it could be ninety feet long. Then came all sorts of natural vegetation, including grass, sage, brush, prickly pear, Spanish dagger, and other plants readily available nearby. After that, farm refuse provided a fuel source with dried corncobs and cornstalks burned as well as hay, sunflower stalks, and even weeds.

Hay evolved as the grassland's major substitute for manure. Hay, though, was a poor alternative for wood because it was a fast-burning fuel. To maximize its burn time, manufacturers developed special hay-burning stoves. Even so, it took a lot of manpower to operate and maintain. The most common hay burner used two thirty-inch-long tubes or magazines filled with compacted hay. These magazines fitted on the side of the firebox, and a spring mechanism at the opposite end of the tube slowly pushed the fuel into the flame. Eight or ten extra magazines had to be filled and ready to insert into the firebox to fuel the flames. An adage at the time said, "It took two men and a boy to keep the hay fire going." Not only was the hay-burning stove labor-intensive, it also increased household fire hazards.

When homesteaders prospered, they could afford to heat with coal, which was a safer fuel by comparison. If the settlers never rose above their initial poverty, they struggled to heat their homes in the winter and cook their food in the summer.

When winter came, David Siceloff's folks in Oklahoma's Cherokee Strip paid him half a cent a day to get up in the mornings and light the fires in the cook stove and the heaters. "I didn't feel abused. Most nine-year-old boys didn't have a steady income."

Though fire and water remained essential to the life of children and their families, both could threaten the survival and comfort of everyone. For instance, because the hay-burning stove required so much fuel, families kept hay inside the house or just outside the door. This could lead to tragic results. The home of the William Bishop family in Dakota Territory burned in 1882 after sparks from a depleted magazine set fire to a nearby supply of hay. The resulting conflagration destroyed their home.

During a frigid winter night a decade later, also in the Dakotas, the Charles and Emilie Schumacher family home suffered a similar fate. The stored straw near their stove caught fire, either from a spark or from spontaneous combustion. The parents and their hired hand gathered up their four blanket-wrapped sons and their eight-day-old daughter Clara in a feather tick and rushed out to their barn for shelter. Only when they reached the barn did they realize the baby was missing. In a panic, the adults raced back to the by-then-blazing home in search of the newborn. They were too late to enter the house, but from the light of the flames spotted the feather tick, which had accidentally fallen into a snow drift. Little Clara was asleep and safe inside the wraps. The Schumachers lost their house, but saved their family.

Terrible though house fires were, prairie fires were even more destructive, a hell on earth. Any fire on the grasslands was dangerous because water was in such short supply, seldom enough to put out a house fire, much less one covering hundreds of acres. Besides the immediate hazard of killing humans and livestock, prairie fires posed a long-term threat to survival. As most prairie fires occurred in the fall after the summer heat and drought had seared the landscape, the blazes destroyed fuel and food humans and animals would need to survive the winter months ahead.

Both nature and man sparked prairie fires. Lightning and spontaneous combustion accounted for some infernos. Human carelessness caused others. An untended campfire, cinders from a passing locomotive, sparks from a fired gun, or a dropped match could start a hellish blaze that threatened everything in its path. With dry grass and foliage for fuel, a small fire with a brisk wind behind it could balloon into a devilish conflagration and race across the prairie.

During a prairie fire, it was everyone's job to protect themselves first and then do whatever they could to stop it. Older children looked after their younger siblings while those big enough to help assisted their parents in fighting the fires, some dousing blankets in water and swatting at flames as they approached a home or barn. Though it was futile to stop the windblown frontal advance of a prairie fire, pioneers attacked the sides of the blaze to keep it from widening. In addition to wet blankets, they sometimes killed a cow and dragged its carcass along the perimeter to snuff out flames. If they had time, they skinned the animal and used the bloody hide like a soaked blanket to beat out the flames of the side fires.

Some settlers in Dakota Territory in the 1880s reported seeing fires far to the north that burned for as long as six weeks, the black smoke at time blotting out the sun for days at a time and filling the air with a stifling aroma of a charred landscape.

Young Kansas girl Adela Richards fought prairie blazes as a child. She remembered the heat and the suffocating smoke as she doused the flames and finally extinguished a modest blaze. "From being the center of a lurid glare, you are suddenly plunged into the bottom of a bucket of pitch. Nothing reflects any light, and there is nothing to steer buy. You don't know where you are, nor where the house is. Everything is black. Your throat is full of ashes and you can hardly breathe for the choking of the fluff in the air."

To protect their homes from prairie blazes, men and their sons would often create a firebreak around their residences. They would plow two separate furrows about fifteen to thirty feet apart and, on a still day, burn the grass and foliage between the parallel ruts. Though not guaranteed to stop a runaway conflagration, the firebreaks offered a degree of protection and reassurance.

Fire also played a role in a natural disaster that nothing could prevent, a plague of grasshoppers. Each year between 1874 and 1877, a horde of grasshoppers carried by strong west winds swooped down upon prairie settlers from northern Texas all the way through Dakota Territory and into Canada. During 1874, the worst plague year, Rocky Mountain locusts descended across the plains, covering an estimated two million square miles of prairie land. At times, they were so thick they blocked out the sun. Wherever they alighted, they devoured crops and the associated hopes of the pioneers.

Settlers across the plains that summer reported first seeing a smoke-like cloud inching across the sun and blotting out the light before arriving in a thunderous buzz of flapping insect wings. A Dakota Territory missionary described their descent upon the ground like "the falling of a snow storm" while Hamlin Garland recalled "the grasshoppers moved in clouds with snap and buzz." Another settler described the noise of their landing on homes and earth like the sound of a continuous hailstorm. In those rare prairie locations with trees, the grasshoppers landed in such numbers that their weight broke large limbs off the trunks. In places, they were reported as much as six inches deep on the ground.

"Are they going to eat us up?" screamed a scared Kansas child at their arrival. While the insects did not consume the children, they terrified the younger ones as they devoured crops and nearly all plant life except for grasses and a few native plants. When settlers realized what was happening, men, women, and older children grabbed shovels and blankets and tried to beat the pests away, but it was like trying to stop the wind with a fishing net. Some families hoped to save critical garden plants by covering them with quilts, blankets, and sheets, but the grasshoppers ate holes in them as well.

Men, women, and older children walked through their fields knocking grasshoppers off their corn stalks, but in their wake could see no effect. Some corn plants were so heavy with the insects that the stalks bent over and the tops touched the ground. One pioneer described the noise of their chomping on the corn as sounding "like a herd of cattle eating in a corn field."

In Shackelford County, Texas, young Sallie Reynolds remembered, "Father had a good crop, and the corn was just coming into roasting ear when an army of grasshoppers came over like a cloud and settled in the field. In a few hours, there was nothing left except the stalks of corn standing like stumps. The other farmers in the country all had the same loss."

The grasshoppers left a hopscotched path of destruction across the Great Plains as they consumed everything at one location. When they had denuded the landscape at one place, the grasshoppers then caught the next wind to ride the air currents to another unlucky site. One Kansas newspaper described their departure with the wording "They rose with such a multitudinous hum of wings as to deepen into a roar like distant thunder, and fled the country."

In their wake, they left a ravaged land, plants little more than nubs; streams and cisterns befouled with their waste; and wooden tool handles so pitted and rough from their ravenous appetites that children could not use them without rubbing their hands raw.

Fourteen-year-old Percy Ebbutt was lowered down his family's hand-dug water well "to clear the hoppers out to keep them from polluting the water" his family drank.

Chickens, turkeys, and pigs ate their fill of the voracious insects, but settlers complained that their meat had the tainted taste of grasshoppers for weeks after their departure. Fish caught in creeks and streams afterwards also had an odd flavor.

When the grasshoppers flew off, they abandoned thousands of their dead behind, leaving a new job for children to rake them into great piles for burning. On other places, children dug small pits to bury the pests in. The only thing good that came out of the 1874 plague was that settlers learned that smoke would drive the grasshoppers away so over the next three years as lesser plagues returned, families with advanced warning built fires to shoo the insects elsewhere. Over the four years of the grasshopper plagues, the locusts devastated an area the size of the eleven states from Maine to Pennsylvania.

Tragic as the plague was, the *Border Sentinel*, in Fort Scott, Kansas, tried to bring a smile to the faces of its readers after the grasshoppers left in August 1874, by printing a parody article from the fictional newspaper *The Grasshopper*. Among the humorous observations, the imaginary newspaper noted, "Grasshopper pot-pie is said to be good. It will make a man jump a mile high," and "A wicked boy says, that 10,000 cats to a family would reduce the grasshopper crop mighty lively." Another item in *The Grasshopper* offered a tongue-in-cheek, yet nauseating cause-and-effect observation: “Sawyer & Mitchell are running their two-story, back-action sausage grinder, day and night, and pay the highest market price for dried and green grasshoppers. Bologna sausage is down to six cents a pound.”

Other than to laugh at their predicament, the settlers had no answer to the insect invasion. The best solution nature offered to the grasshopper plague was a drenching downpour that would drown millions of the pests.

Rain was always a blessing and a curse on the Great Plains. The land remained thirsty because even in the wettest sections of the region, rainfall seldom surpassed twenty inches a year. Too, when it did rain, most precipitations came from thunderstorms that could spawn hail, which devastated crops, or tornadoes that could destroy both crops and homes along with everything inside.

While rain was needed whether to drown grasshoppers or to water crops, it brought certain inconveniences and discomforts to early pioneers, as leakage was the fundamental problem of sod houses, which were the primary structure for prairie homes. A Rooks County, Kansas, sod house saturated with rainwater collapsed in 1880, killing one resident and injuring two.

While such collapses were rare, leakage was a universal challenge for the prairie pioneers. Most of their roofs were sod like the ground the structure was built on because early settlers lacked other building materials. In the best cases, the roofs leaked drips of water, but in the worst cases, streams of mud drained onto the dirt floor. Like their parents, children scurried around their home, positioning pots, pans, pails, and cans to catch the leaking liquid.

The irony of frontier life, especially on the prairies, was that the same families that struggled to find water and fuel for fire could be devastated by it when nature unleashed rains or prairie fires upon them.

Chapter Three

# Vittles and Duds

Vittles and duds ranked with water and fuel as frontier essentials. A common term for food, vittles most often came from the hard labor of pioneers and duds, a slang word for clothing, were often do-it-yourself endeavors involving the whole family. Pioneer children toiled right beside their folks to put food in their bellies and clothes on their backs.

Even with everyone pitching in, the available fare often failed to feed everybody, especially when unexpected mouths arrived for an overnight stay. Six-year-old Peter McBride, who emigrated with his parents to America, recalled stopping at a Utah home for supper one night in 1856. "After the grown folks were through eating, there wasn't any food left, and we children were put to bed hungry. Yes, we were half starved. My little sister Maggie and me cried ourselves to sleep. All my life I have worried for fear my children might get as hungry as I was."

Much of the work in the spring, summer and fall focused on raising and setting aside enough food to get the family through the winter and into the spring.

Then the cycle began again of planting, growing, harvesting, and preserving vegetables and meats for the cold months ahead.

Before the arrival of the railroad and often afterwards in locations distant from railway stops, pioneers had to be self-sufficient except for a few staples like flour, salt, sugar, and coffee. Those they bought from merchants in the nearest town. What they couldn't afford or find, they either made or did without. This created a sparse existence with a diet limited to what they could grow, the edible wild plants they could locate, and the fish and game they could secure.

Born in 1865, Francis Bramlette recalled the self-sufficiency of her childhood south of San Antonio in the years after the Civil War. "We made yeast for our bread.... We raised geese for feathers, manufactured our own clothing, and found a good deal of our food growing wild. It is surprising how many of the wild plants were good to eat."

Self-reliance for pioneers began with the livestock and poultry in the barnyard. Nearly every pioneer home had at least one if not more milch cows to produce milk, a flock of chickens to lay eggs, and a pen of pigs and hogs to supply meat. Each animal meant work for children, sometimes as young as three or four.

When the three oldest boys—Arthur, seven, Edward, five, and Harry, three—of Emilie and Charles Schumacher arrived with their parents in North Dakota in 1888, they immediately handled chores. They gathered eggs, tended chickens, fed pigs, milked cows and churned butter until their younger brother Alfred and baby sister Clara grew old enough to handle those duties. Then the older brothers moved on to more demanding work.

In 1863 Kansas farmer Joseph M. Reed bragged to his brother about his young son. "Little Baz can run all over, fetch up cows out of the stock fields, or oxen, carry in stove wood, and climb in the corn crib, and feed the hogs, and go on errands to his grandma's." Little Baz was only two years and three months old at the time.

Milking cows, a daily task performed each morning and evening, was assigned to young boys and girls. When classes were in session, the children handled the task before and after school. In frontier Iowa, young Hamlin Garland tolerated milking "in pleasant summer weather, when the cows were clean and standing in the open air, but … went to this task in winter with a bitter hatred for the cattle stood in narrow, ill-smelling stalls, close and filthy, especially of a morning."

Like future author Garland, youngster Carl Jones of Merino, Wyoming, loathed milking on frigid winter mornings. After prodding the cow to stand, he would plop his bare feet in the spot where she had lain, as it was the warmest place in the barn. That way, he kept his feet warm while he filled his pail with milk.

After the milking came churning, one of the most despised chores of frontier kids because of its boring tedium. Churning separates cream or whole milk to make butter, which is basically the fat of the milk. Butter was made by hand in a churn, a tapered wooden container with a plunger in the top that children pushed up and down until the liquids separated into their component parts, including butter.

"What a job, that churn!" recalled David Siceloff, a boy in Oklahoma's Cherokee Strip of the 1890s. "The man who invented that instrument of torture must have been an ogre and hated children."

Despite the monotonous churning process that youngsters loathed, butter would last longer than unprocessed milk and could be bartered with neighbors, sold to stores in the nearest community, or exchanged for needed staples and occasional canned goods. Young Siceloff rode nine miles to sell his mother's butter. Producing butter became a closet industry for many frontier families as women and their children made a valuable commodity that sometimes brought in the only cash they might receive for months.

Chickens were another common and valuable source of food and frontier income. Children fed the hens and collected the eggs for their mothers to cook or sell. A hen will lay an average of five eggs a week. The more birds, the more eggs and the more potential meals or sales for the family. When they had a henhouse, children could easily find the eggs. Without a henhouse, kids had to search for the nesting spots of the hens to collect the eggs.

Like butter, surplus eggs were sold or traded. Consequently, "egg and butter money," as it was called, provided "the greater part of their living expenses" for homesteaders such as the Everett E. Harrington family in Kansas. As a boy in Kansas, young Irish emigrant Charles Driscoll remembered the egg and butter money relieved many of his father's financial worries. In the nine months ending in May 1883, Anne Davis, with help from her children, brought in twenty dollars from the sale of forty dozen eggs and fifty-five pounds of butter. Those twenty dollars accounted for sixty percent of the Kansas farm family's cash income during that period.

Once old hens quit laying eggs, pioneers killed them and baked, boiled, roasted, or fried the meat. Older children were tasked with chopping the hen's head off, draining the blood, plucking the feathers, and dressing the carcass, a delicate term for removing the innards. Over their lifetimes of up to ten years, hens provided a lot of eggs and one last meal for the family.

Hogs weighed high in frontier importance as well. While eggs were gathered year round, hogs were slaughtered after the winter's first hard freeze. Swine became an important source of meat on homesteads because they came in large litters, a dozen or more piglets at a time. Their fast growth rate, their appetite for almost anything, and their ability to scrounge around for food made them ideal for the needs of pioneers. Their diet included not only what families fed them but also nuts, roots, grass, plants, berries, and insects, which meant a feast during the grasshopper plagues.

Within three months of birth, a piglet provided with adequate food and water could weigh fifty or more pounds. The same animal at six months, again with plentiful nourishment, might tip the scale at two hundred and fifty pounds. Young swine under a hundred and twenty pounds were called "pigs" while mature swine over that weight were termed "hogs." Shoats were young pigs just after weaning.

The annual process of slaughtering hogs was a lengthy one, involving the whole family for a full day or more, depending on the number of animals processed. After the swine were killed, they were gutted and their hides scalded with boiling water so the bristles or hair could be scraped away. Then the carcass was cut up into various components, including hams, bacon, and fatback. Lesser cuts were ground up into sausage, which was sleeved in casings from the animal's intestines.

Depending on their age, pintsized pioneers helped by doing something as simple as providing wood to keep fires going under wash pots for scalding, as physically taxing as turning the sausage grinder, or as important as sharpening knives for the butchering. Once meat was divided into various cuts, it was salted or put in a smokehouse for preservation in the hopes it would last the family through the winter. Hog-killing also provided some immediate treats, like son-of-a-gun stew, which was made from many of the swine's organs.

Young frontier Texan Frances Bramlette said, "When the hogs were killed, scalded, scraped, cut up and reduced to hams, sausage, middlings, jowls, etc., we always managed to have enough left over to make what is known in west Texas as son-of-a-gun. This was a favorite dish which the family and the neighbors who were invited in to partake enjoyed immensely. I'm very sorry for folks who have never eaten this delicious concoction."

On ranches cattle were available for meat, and wild game abounded everywhere. Where streams or lakes were nearby, fish, turtles, and frogs could be caught. Hunting or fishing, though still work, was one chore young boys and girls enjoyed. They relished the thrill of the hunt, the sense of independence it gave them, and the pride in returning home with food for the table.

Growing up in Oklahoma, Dora Bryant remembered Sunday rabbit hunts were "about the only good time that we ever had." Raised on the Kansas prairies, young Frank Waugh disliked all his chores except hunting. Compared with hunting, he said, "Everything else was as dust in the cyclone."

Depending where the youngsters lived, they might encounter big game like buffalo, deer, antelope, wild hogs, and even bears. Smaller prey included rabbits, ducks, geese, prairie chickens, quail, and turkeys.

Before the Civil War, thirteen-year-old Illinois native Virginia Reed atop her beloved pony, Billy, accompanied her father and other men on buffalo hunts on the Nebraska prairie. She remained amazed at the hulking animals they killed. In Texas a decade after the War Between the States, nine-year-old Don Hamilton Biggers accompanied his father's friend on a search for bison, but never saw a single one.

At four Martha Gay, who grew up in western Missouri, helped her brother Martin, age six, set traps for birds and rabbits and "carried them proudly home." Luna Warner, a Kansas teenager in the 1870s, counted among her quarry rabbits, ducks, turkeys, and even a mired steer she discovered and freed from river mud.

By the age of nine in Dakota Territory near Fort Berthold, James Walker was proficient with "an old muzzle-loading shotgun" and by a year later with a Winchester "pump gun." He and his friend George killed for food and for entertainment. "One time," he recalled of his youthful adventures, "we brought home a big, fat badger … and we had no idea what kind of creature we had killed, but whatever it was we were greatly elated."

Margaret was one of six girls and three boys on the Mitchell homestead in northwest Kansas. "As the girls were older and my father not strong," she recalled later, "the hard toil of the pioneer life fell to the lot of the girls. We used to set traps on the banks of the Republican [River] and caught wolves, badgers, bobcats, and skunks. Wild turkeys were very plentiful then, and we sometimes used traps to catch them."

Besides running traps along the river bank, young Margaret also spent time there fishing. "There were lots of fish in the river, and my sister and I became quite expert in catching them." Fish became a common food source for pioneer families living near watercourses, but not all pioneers were so blessed. Nor had all eaten turtle soup or frog legs, as many pioneers near streams and creeks did for food on the table.

Not all fish were edible, but even so, they might be fed to hogs or discarded in gardens as fertilizer. When shot or trapped game was unsuited for meat, families used the skins or pelts for clothing or trade.

Young Texas girl Sallie Reynolds remembered, "My brothers were fond of hunting and had learned to tan the skins of the deer and antelope. From these Mother made suits for the boys, thus saving herself a lot of weaving. The buckskin was soft when tanned, much like the suede of the present time, although the buckskin would stretch and become stiff and hard if wet."

Besides stalking small game, children—often with their mothers—also hunted plants to supplement their diet when their gardens had yet to produce, or the vegetables they had put up for winter ran out. Depending on the locality, a variety of berries, nuts, and greens were available for the picking when the youngsters knew where and what to look for.

One Colorado girl loved hunting for raspberries, the one chore she didn't have to be threatened to do, because she thrilled at searching for the hidden spots in the meadows and hills where they grew. The search provided a break from the monotony of other chores.

In addition to raspberries, pioneer kids found and picked blackberries, gooseberries, chokeberries, wild grapes, blueberries, elderberries, strawberries, wild plums, and crab apples. They also gathered nuts when the trees dropped them, including hazel nuts, hickory nuts, walnuts, and pecans. Certain green plants like dandelions and lamb's-quarter, a substitute for spinach, were edible when young and tender. Pioneer children learned to recognize those berries, nuts, and plants that added sustenance and variety to their diets.

"Something else which grew wild and was very plentiful was the mustang grape," recalled young Texan Frances Bramlette. "These grapes were not so very good to eat raw, but they made excellent jelly and preserves. The housewives were always glad when it was time for the mustang grapes to come in, for we had very little fruit. Even before they were ripe, we began using them, for the green grapes before the seeds began hardening made wonderful green-grape pies. We children always enjoyed grape-gather[ing] time, for we were allowed to scale the trees and gather the fruit for our elders."

Since nature couldn't provide all a family's needs, a garden became a necessity for pioneers anywhere they lived, whether country or town. The garden marked the intersection of field and kitchen. A productive garden created chores in the kitchen and provided fresh food during the summer and preserved food for the winter.

While the fathers and older sons helped with processing hogs, they left the most of the garden work to their wives and younger children. The garden offered variety to the frontier diet and additional nutrients to keep family members healthy and strong.

Corn became a staple of frontier nutrition because of its versatility in the field and the kitchen. In the field, it was easy to plant, easy to grow with suitable rains, and easy to harvest, just requiring pulling and shucking. Removing the husks and silks was a task easily handled by children. When dried, corn could be ground into meal without threshing as was necessary for wheat and other grains. An 1862 issue of the *Nebraska Farmer* listed thirty-two recipes for corn, including on-the-cob, hominy, corn dodgers, corn muffins, griddle cakes, baked Indian pudding, maize gruel, and cornbread, among others.

In fact, for months at a time, some pioneer families consumed no other type of bread than cornbread, so much so that many children later in life could not stomach the taste of it. Nonetheless, the *Nebraska Farmer* said it was an economical grain. A dollar's worth of corn, according to the journal, provided the same nourishment as two-and-a half dollars of wheat or four dollars of potatoes.

Texas girl Bramlette said, "We grew our own vegetables—sweet potatoes by the ton and lots of pumpkins. To save them through the winter, we built great ricks of cornstalks. We would put mesquite forks in the ground and lay a long ridge pole in the forks. Then we would set cornstalks up against the ridge pole in the shape of the roof of a house until we had the thickness of perhaps twelve inches, and finish by stacking dirt against the corn, beginning at the bottom. When we were through, we had a rick as long as we wanted it, with walls at least a foot and a half thick."

"The next step," she continued, "was to begin piling the potatoes in so they would be next to the back of the rick, and as soon as we had enough to last the family through the winter, we would start rolling in the pumpkins at the front. When the time came to use them, we dug into the front for the pumpkins and into the back for potatoes, carefully covering up the openings with the stalks and dirt each time. In that way, they never froze, and we had the nicest, sweetest potatoes you ever ate, lasting well into the spring. The pumpkins also mellowed and sweetened in their winter den."

In the early years before canning and preserving became a typical household means of storing food for the winter, women, and children dried foods like corn, beans, berries, rhubarb, and pumpkin for later use. They also would store foods in water or brine. Wild plums, for instance, would be gathered, stored in water-filled containers. Though a scum formed on top of the liquid, the plums lasted for months when they could be removed, washed, mashed, sweetened, and made into pies. Though edible, the result was described as "sour and unpalatable." Tomatoes and other vegetables were stored in brine until needed, then removed and soaked in frequently changed fresh water. When the salt was finally leached out, the tomatoes were ready for cooking.

Besides food, the fiber for clothing presented a challenge for pioneers because fabrics were scarce or too expensive for the homestead or ranch budget. For that reason, hides and furs of animals were used for various attire.

Sallie Reynolds, whose brothers killed and tanned hides from deer and other animals, provided a family resource. "My sister became adept at making gloves from this same buckskin, and for these she found ready sale, as cowboys like a nice pair of gloves. They would pay as much as three dollars for a pair of gauntlets with fancy stitching, all of which was done by hand, of course. She also learned to weave hairnets from hair taken from the tails of horses, and with the gray, black and brown, she had a variety of colors to match different heads. These nets were quite popular and the young women would spin and weave for her in exchange for a net."

Cherokee Strip youth David Siceloff remembered an impoverished family whose boys wore "faded and patched waists and pants," and their sisters wore flour sacks "with neck and arm holes." Despite their poverty, they drew respect from their neighbors because they were law-abiding and hard-working folks determined to work their way out of their dire circumstances.

Also in Oklahoma, Susie Crocket did both a man's and a woman's job as a teen, helping her brothers plow and plant their crops and running the thresher and binder at harvest time. She also learned to trap wild animals and tan their hides to bring in more revenue, but she despised sewing. "I hated to see Ma come in with a big batch of sewing, for I knew it meant many long hours sitting by her side sewing seams.... I could help the boys with the plowing or trapping, but they would never help me with the sewing."

While girls and sometimes young boys assisted with clothing tasks, as the males grew older, they worked in other areas, leaving household duties to their female siblings. Field responsibilities, though, were seldom lifted for the girls. Where ready-made clothing or material was unavailable or costly, families recycled what they had or made cloth from fibers, whether cotton or wool, in a time- and labor-intensive process.

While the Reynolds family in Texas used tanned hides from their boys' hunting, the Applegate family children for years wore overcoats made from the canvas cover of the wagon that had delivered them to Oregon's Willamette Valley. When clothes wore out, pioneer mothers and their daughters would unstitch the seams and salvage usable material to make outfits for the smaller children.

The pioneers reused all the cloth they could because the process for making clothes from scratch required time, patience, and skill. If they used homegrown cotton or wool, the fiber had to first be picked from the plant or sheared from the animal. Then the fiber had to be cleaned of seeds, burrs, and trash. The resulting fiber was then carded to straighten the strands so they could be spun into thread. The thread then had to be woven into cloth and dyed for sewing into functional attire.

"To dress in style was not thought of in those days," according to Alzada Baxter, who grew up on the Kansas prairies. Fashion wasn't as important as just having acceptable clothes to begin with.

Repairing garments accounted for many sewing tasks, with girls especially helping their mothers knit stockings, darn socks, patch shirts and pants, and stitch quilts together from fabric scraps too small to use for anything else. Often these chores occurred in the evening after all the cooking and housework had been done. When time and materials permitted, the daughters and their moms stitched curtains for the windows, embroidered linens for the tables, stuffed feathers into pillow ducking, and fashioned lap robes for cold winter nights.

So critical was providing clothing for the family that the first labor-saving device in most homes was a treadle sewing machine, which cut hours out of the production time. Young Frances Bramlette in Texas thought it was a red-letter day in her family's life when their dad purchased one for a hundred dollars.

"Father bought us a Wheeler and Wilson sewing machine," little Frances later recalled. "I remember distinctly the day the sewing machine agent came to the house with that wonderful machine and gave us a demonstration, showing what beautiful ruffles it could gather, what lovely small tucks it could make, and what a remarkable quilter it had with which our sunbonnets could be quilted so easily."

Neighbors came from miles around to see the appliance and then brought sewing jobs for the family to handle. As her mother's eyes deteriorated, making it difficult for her to keep up with the workload, "Father decided he would take over. He thought it would be great fun to sew with a machine…. Anyway, he got a lot of kick out of running the machine," though he wasn't eager for his male friends to learn of his womanly skills. After the newness wore off, Frances's father tired of the task, and the machine stayed idle until Frances and her sister grew enough to work the treadle. After that, they did the family sewing until they left home.

When Lily Klasner moved with her folks from Texas to New Mexico in 1866, she remembered her mother's fussiness over one device. "There was one piece of equipment which Mother was very proud, and which required careful packing—her sewing machine. I am sure that she had a good supply of needles, thread, buttons, and other equipment for sewing, for I well remember her using them after we reached our home."

Another problem with attire was shoes. They were expensive and wore out quickly from daily work and chores. Consequently, most children and many adults went without shoes during the warm months and sometimes even in winter. On many occasions, they used improvised footwear, tacking tanned leather or rawhide atop wooden soles to provide primitive footwear. Socks were scarce unless knitted by women folks, so sometimes children and men wore rags around their feet when they needed socks.

When early settlers did have a set of good clothing or one pair of store-bought shoes, they mostly wore them only on special occasions, like church or dances and other socials. No stigma was attached to the clothing deficiency, as most of their neighbors faced the same situation.

With time, though, the challenges of providing vittles and duds lessened, easing the workload on children. First of all, as pioneers established their farms and ranches, they gradually grew more prosperous. With prosperity they had more disposable income to buy labor-saving devices like sewing machines. Those mechanisms failed to eliminate the tasks, but made them more manageable and saved time in the long run.

Second, the nation with time prospered as well because of the industrial revolution, which mass-produced goods at a lower price. With the expansion of the railroads, those consumer items could reach more and more communities, even in some of the nation's most isolated places. As isolation shrank for the pioneers, their prosperity grew.

As affluence broadened, the difficulties and the time needed to provide fuel, water, vittles, and duds lessened. This freed children to take on other tasks, including their own education. They may have started frontier life in dire circumstances that required their work for survival, but they never shirked from the task or thought themselves the worse for it.

Years after his Kansas pioneer child upbringing, Charles Driscoll summed up a common perception at the time, saying, "We never considered ourselves poor people."

That attitude was exemplified by a Morton County, Kansas, woman who identified herself as "P.E.T." in a letter to the *Harper* (Kansas) *Sentinel* in 1889. She explained she lived in a dugout twelve-by-twenty feet in size with a white-washed ceiling and a canvas partition with her husband and two sons as well as "a canary bird to sing to me, a pet skunk, a dog, and a cat." Though her husband farmed, "this year everything was a failure in this county" and he hauled freight to keep the family afloat.

"Last spring," she wrote, "everything was fine; good prospects for plenty in the fall; but the hot winds came, and the rain did not. Out of the eighty acres of spring crops we planted, we got nothing but corn stalks, not an ear of corn or a kernel for seed. We may be thankful for the stalks, as some did not even get stalks."

In her husband's absence hauling freight, P.E.T. and her boys shared the workload. "We are forty-seven miles from the railroad, and the only way to get a living is to freight. It takes four days to go to the railroad and back with a load. My man has gone for a load now. While he is gone, I take care of thirteen head of cattle, two pigs, one colt, and milk four cows, do my housework, make lace and crazy patch. This morning I sawed a new stove-pipe hole through the roof and put up tin to run the pipe out through [while] the boys are at school."

She continued, "Times are hard, but I am generous, and when you come 'out west,' just stay a while at our dugout. You shall have pancakes and meat grease for breakfast—maybe a little coffee. Light bread for dinner and mush and milk for supper the year round, with occasionally a young jackrabbit fried with some milk gravy."

A pintsized Dakota Territory pioneer described early settlers as falling into two categories: the "shirkers and quitters" and the "workers and stickers." P.E.T. was a worker and a sticker, like her sons.

So, too, were the boys and girls of the time, largely because they had no choice. They did what their parents told them. Without realizing it, they helped tame the west by contributing their labor to putting food on the table and clothes on their backs. Even when they left home, sometimes at an age contemporary Americans would find unbelievable, they were better prepared to fend for themselves because of all the tasks they had learned to handle from the time they were mere toddlers.

Chapter Four

# House and Barn

Once pioneer families arrived at their destinations, building shelter became their long-term focus. Most settlers started from scratch to erect cover for themselves and eventually for their livestock.

In forested regions where timber was plentiful, starting a log cabin required an ax, a saw, and plenty of muscle. If they were lucky, a family might have settled near a sawmill that offered finished lumber for a frame house. Such milled lumber eased the labor, but not always the cost of building a home because nails were expensive. However, on the prairie, where traditional construction materials were scarce, erecting a house involved ingenuity.

Pioneers also considered cost. A modest frame house in 1860 could run two hundred and fifty dollars, compared to a sod house that might cost between a dollar and a quarter and fifty dollars. Whatever the environment or the price, construction was a long and laborious process involving the whole family, using what few tools and building supplies they had squeezed into their wagons with everything else they needed to start a new life in the wilderness.

Even when completed, the shelter was crude, cramped, and uncomfortable, especially during inclement weather. A pioneer west Texas boy said the only word that truly described the family home was "snug." Quarters were so tight that women often joked they could fix breakfast without getting out of bed, and a Montana mother claimed she had flipped flapjacks on the kitchen stove from her bedroom. Housing remained crowded until families could harvest a crop and establish some financial flexibility that permitted them to improve and ultimately expand their homes.

And the tasks of keeping house were unending and exhausting for children. Little prairie girl Hattie Lee looked back on her childhood chores through unsentimental eyes. "No one," she said, "can tell the hardships I went through; carry water from the well; rub the clothes on a washboard; and keep the housework up…. They never thought a young girl ever got tired."

On the northern plains, sod houses were built from earthen bricks interlaced with roots, which held them together. These earthy building blocks were cut from the land by special "breaking plows," trimmed a uniform size, and then stacked grass-side down in twin and overlapping rows to make walls as high as eight feet. A strong ridge pole provided the basis for the roof and supported rafters which held the roofing material. If available and affordable, tarpaper was laid over the rafters to provide a more effective leakage barrier. Most pioneers, however, had no choice but to use the same earthen sod for the roof as they had used for the walls.

On the south plains where the soil was less cohesive and the grassroots were not as substantial, settlers built dugouts in the hillsides. They excavated a square plot in a hill or a rise, shaping three dirt walls for their new home. The builders would then close in the front of the hole with a stone or wooden wall and next build a roof—of wood if it was available or sod if it was not—over the excavation. Wood was seldom accessible for a floor, so families improvised. Whether a dugout or a sod house, the dwellings had a single door, but few if any windows, keeping them dark during the day. The primary advantage of a dugout or soddy was that they remained cooler in the summer and warmer in the winter than a log or frame house.

Soddies and dugouts may have provided shelter, but they were imperfect cover, little different from living in a hole in the ground like a prairie dog. Rain and snow created leaks in the roofs, adding to the discomfort. Beyond that, all sorts of crawly creatures made a home out of the sod house, regardless of the moisture or the weather.

Seepage came with the rain and the snow, usually continuing days after the sun had reappeared. The problem could be as annoying as drips or as devastating as streams of "yellow mud," as one young Kansas pioneer remembered. Because of the weight of rain-saturated sod, families often had to brace their ceiling ridge poles and rafters to prevent roofs from caving in.

Though total collapses occurred on occasion, the inconvenience of rains to the residents of soddies or dugouts was constant because the roofs on most soddies consisted of sod and dirt, like the walls because suitable roofing materials were so scarce or expensive. Oklahoma youth David Siceloff described the problem simply: "A sod roof will take just so much water, and then it leaks."

Some families collected tin cans that the children flattened for makeshift shingles that would deflect water rather than absorb it. Every family put out dishpans and other containers to catch the water and prevent it from muddying the floors. Those preparations seldom caught all the water, leaving the dwelling as muddy as the outdoors in the downpour.

The Vincent and Mary Kahle family in 1887 Wallace County, Kansas, lived in a sod house with a dirt roof. Ten days after Mary gave birth to one of their children, a three-day deluge began. The dwelling leaked so badly that they rolled up their bedding, bound it with a rope, and put it on the dinner table beneath an oil cloth to keep it dry. Mary put her newborn atop the rolled mattresses and held an umbrella over the baby to keep her dry. "Soon," Mary remembered, "the rain ran off the ribs of the parasol and soaked around the baby so I fixed a place for her in the cupboard shelf, the only dry place in the house. I walked around with a slicker, a man's hat and overshoes to keep dry…." One of her goals for herself and her family was to one day live in "a house that didn't leak."

Young Rosetta Singley in western Kansas remembered her mother trying to catch the initial drips after a summer thunderstorm released a deluge on the earthen-floored sod house. The drips became streams, and the streams became floods through every crack in the house. "Soon water was standing all over the floor, filling the holes that had been swept out since March. Practically everything was wet," she recalled, including her toddler brother Carl, who was caked with mud from crawling around on the floor.

One young Kansas girl remembered her father's dugout. "When it rained, the water came through the roof and ran in the door. After the storms, we carried the water out with buckets, then waded around in the mud until it dried up."

A visitor to a Dakota Territory homestead watched as the lady of the house retrieved her old dishes, her pots, and her pans and positioned them on the stove, the floor, and the furniture, preparing for an approaching storm cloud. Some families put their infants into dry-goods crates to protect them or had older children hold an umbrella or other covering over them. One Ness County, Kansas, family had lined their ceiling with flour sacks, but the facing still leaked. The best the parents and children could do was jab table forks into the lining to direct the streams of water toward various containers on the furniture or on the floor. Once water filled the pots and pans, older children quickly emptied them outside to be filled again.

One Kansas mother and her offspring escaped their leaking home for a neighbor's dugout, only to leave it the next morning when rainwater stood six inches on the floor. The family waited out the rainstorm beneath a sheath of boards propped against a wall.

Even when the rain ended outside, ceilings continued to leak inside for several days after the sun reappeared. Once the downpours stopped and the sun emerged, boys and girls helped their parents carry garments and belongings out into the sunshine, hanging their possessions on clothes lines and spreading them on grass and bushes to dry. A saturating rain also soaked into the walls, loosening the plaster or muslin cloth or newspapers women had used to hide the dirt surface and make the sod house interior more livable. The wall coverings would fall off in strips or in their entirety, leaving cleanup tasks often given to the children so the parents could repair the damage.

The earthen materials that allowed rain and snow melt to drain into the house also provided easy access for insects, rodents, lizards, and snakes. These creatures made the dwelling their home as well.

Snakes, of course, were the most terrifying and, in the case of rattlesnakes, the most dangerous intruders. The legless reptiles fell from the ceiling or crawled through gaps in the walls, hiding wherever they could. Alerted by her barking dog, young mother Mary Kahle investigated a pair of shoes in the corner of her soddy. As she neared the footwear, a rattlesnake poked its head out of one.

The James Germann children who lived near the Kansas-Colorado border one day played a prank on their mother by hiding their baby sibling behind a curtain in a corner cupboard. Bewildered at the lost infant, their mother panicked until, as one prankster recalled, "Mother heard the rattle of a snake, and sure enough, there it was right beside the baby." Mrs. Germann rescued her baby unharmed, killed the snake, and in an immediate search of the house found another rattler wrapped around a bedpost.

As a girl in Kansas, Mary Northway was combing her hair when a nonvenomous blue racer, a dark snake that can grow up to four and a half feet, dropped from the ceiling to the floor between her and the mirror. For weeks after that experience, she "imagine[d] I could see snake heads sticking through the roof in different places." In addition to the sheets on their beds, some pioneer families tied sheets over their beds to keep snakes from falling on them as they slept. One of Mary Northway's Osborne County, Kansas, girlfriends recalled, "It was nothing to be surprised to look up at the ridge log in our little sod house and see a snake watching you, or one sticking his head out from between the roof and the wall."

Another Kansas girl recalled that "sometimes the bull snakes would get in the roof, and now and then, one would lose his hold and fall down on the bed, then off on the floor. Mother would grab the hoe … and after the fight was over, Mr. Bull Snake was dragged outside."

Besides snakes, some pests like scorpions, centipedes, and spiders could be dangerous with their bites and stings. Other pests included fleas, bedbugs, ants, flies, gnats, roaches, mice, rats, and other vermin. Kansas girl Dee Posey remembered she slept with two siblings "and I don't know how many bedbugs." Children used brooms to kill what insects they could, but fleas and bedbugs had to be squashed between fingernails, a task often given to the little girls in the family.

Between snakes, bugs, and grit falling from the ceiling and walls, young Coloradoan Anne Ellis one day had had enough. She fled to a hill, lay down in the grass on her back, and gazed wide-eyed at the sky, comforted "knowing that nothing dirty would drop into my eyes."

Frank Baker, a Kansas homesteader who dubbed himself the "Lane County Bachelor" made light of the situation with a verse he adapted to the melody of "The Irish Washerwoman:"

*How happy I feel when I crawl into bed,*
*And a rattlesnake rattles a tune at my head.*
*And the gay little centipede void of all fear,*
*Crawls over my neck and down into my ear.*
*And the gay little bedbugs so cheerful and bright,*
*They keep me a-laughing two-thirds of the night.*
*And the gay little flea with sharp tacks on his toes,*
*Plays, 'Why don't you catch me' all over my nose.*

In addition to all the uninvited guests, during harsh winter months families sometimes squeezed their milk cow, young calves, chickens, and other fragile animals inside their cramped quarters to keep them from freezing to death outside.

With a drafty, leaky roof, with earthen walls that spawned bugs and reptiles, and with the occasional stay of some barnyard animals, good housekeeping in a sod house presented a challenge. One pintsized pioneer summed up the predicament by saying "Mother disliked sweeping her floor with a hoe."

It's hard to keep a house clean and presentable when the floors, the walls and even the roofs consist of dirt. Even so, pioneer women tried, creating additional tasks for themselves and their children as they made their dwellings more livable, no matter how meager their circumstance was, like that of Kansas matron Margaret Raser.

In the late 1870s in Hodgeman County, Raser surveyed her single-room sod home. Her kitchen included a small stove, a homemade cupboard, a swill bucket, a box for buffalo chips, a rack for towels, kitchen utensils hanging on nails, and a bench for the family washbasin and water bucket. A cradle, beds high enough to slide a trundle bed beneath, a bureau, two trunks, a rocking chair, and coal-oil lamps for illumination made up the furniture. The family washtub, dishpan, and boiler hung on nails on the outside wall. That was all.

With their children's help, women improvised to make their quarters more homey. In the evenings, they made rag rugs from worn-out or tattered cloth to cover their floors. Some families created wall-to-wall rag carpets they stretched over a layer of straw and tacked to their earthen floors. While the covering presented a more inviting floor, it collected dust and had to be removed periodically and taken outside for a beating to dislodge the dirt. Too, if the roof leaked, the carpet would be untacked and dragged outside to dry, then returned inside, a laborious task requiring most of the family's belongings to be moved as well.

Other families used hides from cattle and buffalo for floor coverings. Some households spread salt and other concoctions on the floor to harden it and make it more water resistant. Whatever their approach, the task fell most often to women and children.

For wall coverings, children helped their mothers tack plain muslin cloth, brightly colored strips of gingham or even old newspapers to the dirt surfaces. Though less attractive than the cloth, the newspaper coverings also offered children a resource to learn their A-B-C's and to read.

To add color to the room, women, and their daughters in the evenings sewed shapes of fabrics together to make patchwork quilts to drape over beds built on wooden frames. Boys often filled cloth sacks or ticks, as they were called, with straw or cornhusks for mattresses.

With wood scarce for any use, pioneer families re-purposed dry-goods boxes as tables or bureaus and adapted crates or worn-out kegs as chairs. While traveling trunks might hold clothing, they also served as improvised benches, crude cupboards, or cradles for newborns.

Whatever the nightly chores after supper, they all required light in the cabin. In the early years of the homestead era, many families relied solely on candles. Young Annie Gilkeson of Kansas remembered, “We had only tallow candles for light, and one of my duties was to make them each week. The mold held one dozen, and that was sufficient for the time.”

Tallow was lard rendered from meat, most commonly after hogs were slaughtered. Melted tallow was poured into the candle molds after a wick or string was inserted. The wick in a candle drew fuel by capillary action to the flame, which provided a modest glow of illumination for the cabin. Interior lighting improved with the introduction of coal-oil and kerosene lamps into the homes. Children often maintained those light fixtures. Their tasks included trimming the scorched tips from the wicks, filling the lamp reservoirs with fuel, and cleaning the glass globes or chimneys of the smoke residue.

Texas girl Sallie Reynolds remembered, “The coal-oil lamps gave a much brighter light than candles. In fact, with a shade, they gave an excellent light for reading.”

Not only was tallow an important light source, it also kept families and their clothes clean. Along with lye, animal lard was the key ingredient in the homemade soap used for washing hands, taking baths, and doing laundry. One common chore of boys and girls involved collecting the ashes from stoves, fireplaces, and other fires on the homestead to produce lye.

Children saved the ashes in a keg until time to make the soap, then leached lye from the ashes. Wood ashes were best, but cornstalk ashes often substituted on the prairie. Sallie Reynolds described the process, saying "The ashes were put in a crude sort of hopper made of barrel staves on boards with the ends set together and slanting upward and outward making a trough-like receptacle, wide at the top and narrow at the bottom, which was filled with ashes. Water was poured on this until the ashes were saturated and began to drip. This carrying water was a slow, tedious task, which my brothers hated."

San Saba County, Texas, girl Sarah Harkey, remembered "all preparations were made for winter, which consisted of gathering sweet potatoes and pumpkins and holding them up, and hog killing, rendering out lard, then carrying water to run lye to make up soap for winter, which was a task that fell on the small children. It was one hopper of ashes after another. We had to drip until all the soap was made."

The resulting lye-water was collected in a huge wash pot, then boiled with the tallow and possibly skillet drippings, fat scraps, and even candle ends. Children fed the fire and the older ones helped their mother stir the pot. The task was hard and hot as well as uncomfortable because the lye fumes were irritating to the eyes and nose. Depending on how much fat was put in and how long it boiled, the resulting concoction, when cooled, had the consistency of a thick jelly good for laundering clothes and cleaning dishes. If salt was added, and the mixture was boiled longer, and then allowed to harden in bread pans, cake soap resulted, suitable for bathing and washing hands.

Just as making soap was a long and tedious task, so was using that soap to do laundry. Living in a prairie dwelling made of the same soil that the family worked in the fields meant that clothes quickly grew filthy. Washing clothes was time-consuming and laborious, involving the women, the children and occasionally the men.

Some pioneers like young Texan Frances Bramlette were fortunate to live near a watercourse where on wash days several families would gather at a creek to do their laundry. Though the men would help build the fires and carry water to wash pots, their principal duty was to watch for Indians while their wives and kids did the work.

"The men had made a bench of a split oak tree with the top side hewn off and planed smooth," Frances recalled. "On this the women placed the articles to be washed, especially the men's heavy shirts, jeans, trousers, and underwear, and pounded them with a paddle-shaped piece of wood made out of heavy lumber. The bench was called the battling bench, and the paddle was known as the battling board. It seems as if they would have battered the clothes all to pieces, but that was the way they did it—just pounded to beat the band, sometimes calling in the men folks to help them battle."

Doing laundry with neighbors reduced the tedium, but for most prairie families "wash day" remained a long, laborious chore, so much so that one pioneer mother said the event should be renamed "wash days."

The task started with boiling water with soft soap, then dumping the clothes in the hot liquid and prodding them with a broom handle. After a while in the broth, the clothes were removed and taken to a wooden block. There the mother or one of her older daughters pounded the clothes to loosen the grime, then rinsed the garment again. This process was repeated multiple times until the item was deemed clean. The major concern in this process was to not damage any buttons, since they were costly and scarce on the frontier.

The laundry crew then hung the garments on a clothesline, if one was available, or draped them over bushes or grass to dry. Later, washboards and other inventions did away with the mallet pounding, but required the workers to agitate the clothing in hot water. Ironing was equally exhausting, especially since flatirons weighed ten or more pounds and had to be heated on a hot stove. Montana youth Llewellyn Callaway remembered the most "irksome tasks" of his boyhood were "getting the wood, washing dishes, washing diapers, ironing, and wheeling the baby carriage" when he was out of school.

The point Callaway made about wheeling the baby carriage raised a common complaint among older frontier siblings, that of having to take care of their younger brothers and sisters. With everyone having to contribute to the family's survivors, mothers often assigned their oldest children, especially the senior daughters, to look out for their little siblings.

A daughter of the Nebraska prairies and later a successful American author, Mari Sandoz believed that "often there was no difference in the work done by the boys and the girls, except that the eldest daughter of a sizeable family was often a serious little mother by the time she was six."

The oldest of eight children, west Texas farm girl Ruth, years after she married and moved from her parents' place, answered a query about why she never had children. "By the time I left home," she replied, "I had already raised one family."

Texas native Lily Klasner, who grew up in New Mexico Territory, was the third of nine offspring of Robert Adam and Ellen Eveline Casey. "For years," she recalled in adulthood, "there was always a baby in the home whose care was my evening work. I loved my little brothers and sisters, but at times resented the responsibility for them. Ellen (her older sister) was supposed to help with this, but she was not strong, and seldom did much to assist me."

When she was almost five, Lily remembered caring for her little brother John. "As I stood by his cradle rocking him to sleep, I saw a large centipede crawl over the end of the pillow toward his head. Before I could stop it, the centipede was in the baby's hair. I knocked it off and screamed. Both Mother and Grandmother, who lived with us, rushed to me. Mother was armed with the fire tongs and Grandmother with the poker. I pointed to the horrible crawling thing that had regained the pillow. Mother seized it with the tongs, mashed its head and carried it out of doors."

Young Nebraska boy George MacGinitie remembered the worst responsibility he ever had was holding watch over his sleeping baby brother and swishing the flies away from him. "In all my life," he recalled, "I think I have never had a task so disagreeable.... Some time I would 'accidentally' waken Henry by brushing his face, and when Mother came to get him, I would take out on a dead run for the ... pond" to go swimming.

Sometimes necessity required children to assist with childbirth. A twelve-year-old Texas daughter faced that situation when her mother went into labor with her father absent. That night the little girl helped her mother deliver a stillborn baby, then found a small crate to bury her tiny sibling in before her younger brothers and sisters awoke and discovered the tragedy.

Not all childbirths ended so tragically. Frontier doctors were scarce, and the oldest daughter often had to help deliver her younger siblings. By some accounts, few girls reached adulthood on the frontier without having witnessed the birthing of at least one child. If the newborn survived, it meant long-term chores for the baby's older sisters, including watching out for them.

The older children not only protected their younger siblings, but changed their diapers, fed them, and monitored them when their mothers were otherwise occupied. Like young Lily Klasner, not all enjoyed the tasks, which could be simply boring or frustrating.

Comparable to changing diapers, perhaps the most unsavory task that fell to children in pioneer homes was emptying the chamber pots or "slop jars." Chamber pots were vessels that individuals used when they needed to relieve themselves during the night or during weather too bitter to step outside to the outhouse. As they got old enough to carry the slop jars to the outhouse and dump the waste in the pit, both young boys and girls handled the task.

The children also managed cleaning the animal waste from barns and chicken coops. North Dakotan Stephanie Prepiora and her siblings cleaned dung from their farm shelters, as did Iowans Mary Rebecca Williams, twelve, and her nine-year-old brother, George. By removing droppings and replacing soiled straw for animal bedding, the children maintained a clean environment for their livestock and poultry. Cleanliness in the barn kept animals healthier and minimized the incursion of pests.

Often the first farm building a pioneer family built was a small hay shed to provide cover for the hay or grain a family would need to get their livestock through the winter months. Another early addition to the farm buildings was a chicken coop where the birds could roost and nest. Too, the chickens could be secured in the coop at night, reducing the chance of coyotes and other varmints killing them. Further, a coop made it easier for the children to collect eggs since they were in one place, compared to the impromptu nests of free-range chickens.

The irony of a prosperous prairie farm was that when the family could afford it, they built a new house. When they did, they transformed their original sod house into a barn for their livestock. Poor though the soddy may have been as a human habitation, it was still too valuable a resource on the homestead to be abandoned.

For all the faults and shortcomings of frontier housing, it was still home for families as articulated by young Nebraskan Will Cox in the late 1860s when he moved into his home after first starting a garden and planting crops on their new homestead. "Sometime in August we occupied our new 'residence.' … Of course our house was incomplete … but it was surely home sweet home compared with living outdoors for nearly five months."

Chapter Five

# Soil and Toil

For the adults, particularly the men, the land became the attraction. The frontier offered them a chance to claim a plot for their own. In their eyes, property was the key to future prosperity for themselves and their offspring. In the eyes of their wondrous children, the land was both a playground to explore and a work site to endure.

As most Americans lived on farms until late in the nineteenth century, farm work drew youngsters into the fields to help their parents plant, grow, and harvest the crops that provided a marketable commodity and gardens that put food on the table.

Young Edna Matthews spent her childhood on a frontier Texas farm that grew corn and cotton. She dreaded autumn when harvesting began. Pulling corn ears was hard enough, but picking cotton was the worst in the heat of late August and early fall. She remembered that the corn and cotton fields towered "like a monster" before her. The tedious task of harvesting challenged her. "Sometimes I would lie down on my sack and want to die," she recalled decades later. "Sometimes they would pour water over my head to relieve me."

As difficult a challenge as it was facing the dreaded monster, Edna understood it had to be defeated. "It was instilled in us that work *was* necessary. Everybody worked; it was a part of life, for there was no life without it."

Whether the family settled in the forested regions or on the treeless plains, the chores began as soon as they arrived at their new homes. In areas with trees, the timber had to be felled, and the stumps grubbed up to prepare land for cultivation. On the prairie, the thick sod—tightly embedded with grassroots—had to be broken with turning plows. The resulting clods and clumps of earth had to be crushed to provide the loose soil needed for planting. Though necessary, the chore remained tedious and boring.

Young Mary Alice Zimmerman helped her father break the land on their Kansas homestead. "The soil was virgin," she remembered. "It had to be broken, turned, stirred, and taught to produce." Teaching the land to produce took work.

After first breaking the sod of his new field, an Oklahoma homesteader set his family to work pulverizing acres of clods. He and his wife used axes to bust up the clumps while his three children went at the task with butcher knives.

Another Oklahoma pintsized pioneer remembered a similar process for the family garden. David Siceloff said, "Mother wanted a garden, so a patch was plowed near the house. The sod was hacked and chopped in shreds. The shreds were tumbled about, beaten and shaken. The roots and grass were raked off and beds made. Seeds were planted and—lo!—there was a garden."

Young David made it sound so simple, but growing a successful garden, much less a crop, required extensive effort. Once the land was cleared in forested regions or the sod broken on the prairie, the process began with plowing.

Prairie offspring and later author Hamlin Garland remembered the first time he was called on by his father to plow as it "seemed a very fine and manly commission." He recalled the vast pride in plowing his first furrow a half mile from side to side of their hundred-and-sixty-acre farm, then reality set in. "The pride and elation did not last," he wrote. "The task soon became exceedingly tiresome and the field lonely. It meant moving to and fro, hour after hour, with no one to talk to and nothing to break the monotony. It meant walking eight or nine miles in the forenoon and as many more in the afternoon, with less than an hour off at dinner. It meant care of the [plow] share (the cutting edge)—holding it steady and properly. It meant dragging the heavy implement around the corners, and it meant also many mishaps where thick stubble or wild buckwheat rolled up around the standard and threw the share completely to the ground."

To fight his boredom, he whistled, sang, and studied the clouds. He watched the prairie chickens as they gathered or a hawk sailing overhead or a passing flock of geese. At his feet, he looked at the mice, lizards, and gophers whose nests and little granaries of seeds he had obliterated. Occasionally, he thought he saw the specter of a shadowy wolf.

When Garland first began plowing, he was so short that he had to reach above his shoulders to grab the implement's handles. People passing on the road sometimes stopped, and he could hear them say, "That's a little too young a boy to do work like that."

Garland was not alone. "I have plowed acre after acre from the time I was twelve years old," Percy Ebbut of Kansas remembered. Oklahoma girl Fannie Eisele started plowing at age eleven and with her brother plowed the hundred and sixty acres of their homestead. Up in North Dakota, R.D. Crawford, also eleven years old, plowed three square miles of land—1,920 acres—his first year behind a plow. Over the next dozen years, Crawford estimated—perhaps exaggerated—he had trailed behind a plow for almost 30,000 miles.

Oklahoman David Siceloff remembered when his father hooked up the plow to the mule team and put the lines over his shoulder. "See if you can plow," his dad told him, pointing to the field that had been plowed many times previously. "It's easy," his father said. Young David tried it. He recalled years later, "The plow stood up most of the time without any help and the mules knew how to plow. At the end of the field, they turned and came back exactly as they should … It was fun at first, but after a few rounds, the fun seeped away, and I followed listlessly behind the plow."

Beyond the plowing and soil preparation in spring, farm families after the harvest often plowed up the fields again to turn the stubble over into the soil so the decaying plant matter would return nutrients back to the acreage. Prairie boy Hamlin Garland said in the fall months he would "day after day … follow his team in the field, turning over two acres of stubble each day…. His heart was sometimes very bitter and rebellious because of the relentless drag of his daily toil. It seemed that the stubble land miraculously restored itself each night. His father did not intend to be cruel, but he was himself a hard-working man, an early riser, and a swift workman, and it seemed a natural and necessary thing to have his sons work. He himself had been bound out at nine years of age and had never known a week's release from toil."

The tedium of the stubble plowing grew on young Garland until he looked forward to the approaching cold winter months when "the plow was brought in, cleaned and greased to prevent its rusting, and upturned in the tool shed."

With such continued tilling year after year, the large clods and clumps that hindered planting were gradually pulverized, making the fields easier to work. After the sod was first broken, farming evolved into a cyclical routine of plowing, planting, cultivating, harvesting and plowing again. Once the field had been plowed in the spring and the soil prepared for sowing, the pioneers put in their crops. Corn was a favored crop on the plains because it was easy to plant and easy to harvest, as compared to grains like wheat and sorghum. Further, it was versatile, providing solid nourishment for family and livestock.

Although children and adults often joined to plant corn crops, sometimes the chore was left to the children alone out of necessity. In early fields still lumpy from their newness, children carried a stick or pole to stab into the soil. Then a child would drop a kernel of corn in the hole. A trailing sibling would cover the hole. As the soil was pulverized and the soil loosened from multiple crops over the years, a child who went barefoot could use a big toe to create the hole for the kernel. Some youngsters developed such skill that they seldom missed dropping a seed into the hole.

Sometimes, though, the planting went awry when the children didn't understand the task. Young Mary Alice Zimmerman recalled one such boo-boo from her childhood. "Father sent me out one spring day to plant castor beans along the hedge to keep the moles away. He gave me about one gallon of seeds and a sharpened stick. As I look back now, I think it was to have been an all-day job; but, thanks to my ignorance, I found that I could press the stick quite deep into the wet soil, thus could put a lot of seeds in one hole, so was soon through. I never will forget the queer smile on his face when I returned with the empty bag."

Sowing wheat was a greater challenge than planting corn or even castor beans, as it had to be broadcast or thrown by hand on a prepared field. That skill took time to develop because the seeds needed to be evenly dispersed over the soil. So, adults scattered the seeds with their children following behind them using rakes or dragging a flat piece of lumber to cover the wheat seeding with soil.

In addition to their fields, pioneers also planted gardens to provide vegetables that could be eaten in season. Some of the summer produce was conserved for later use, either being stored in cool root cellars or being preserved in various canning processes. Depending on location, typical garden fare included potatoes, pumpkins, melons, cabbage, squash, beans, peas, sweet potatoes, tomatoes, carrots, cucumbers, and others. While the gardens were smaller than the commercial crops grown in the fields, they remained critical to the family's survival.

Once the crops were sown, the chores changed for the children. One of their critical tasks was assuming the role of living scarecrows to scare off livestock from trampling fields, birds from eating seeds, and rodents from digging up seeds or eating new growth.

Matilda Peitzke, who grew up on an Iowa homestead, recalled how she and her siblings "had to stay out in the field and chase blackbirds" so they wouldn't scratch out seed corn to devour or eat the young sprouts. Matilda and her young brothers and sisters also guarded the family livestock "to keep them out of other people's as well as out of our own fields."

An infestation of pocket gophers struck Albany County, Wyoming, in 1888, not only threatening crops but also horses and cattle. Gopher holes were easy for livestock to step in and break their legs. The problem was so great that the county put up a bounty of a nickel for each gopher scalp turned in to officials. Both boys and girls hunted the burrowing rodents for the rewards. Young Minnie Rietz followed her cat around and whenever it snared a gopher, she would borrow the prey long enough to clip a part of its scalp. After she returned the kill to her pet, she pocketed the hide and later a nickel for each one she delivered.

Besides guarding fields and gardens from animals, frontier kids also protected them from weeds that stole nutrients and sketchy moisture from the soil that grew the crops. Children either pulled the unwanted plants or chopped them with hoes.

Growing up in western Kansas, Blanche Beal and her brothers enjoyed planting a garden because they could work with their father, but they detested hoeing and weeding the vegetable patch without him. The potato crop became the bane of the Driscoll brothers, also of Kansas. "We boys hated the potato crops more than any other thing on the farm," remembered Charles Driscoll. First, they had to plant the potato seed and then hoe the patch. When the plants bloomed, they had to pick or knock off potato bugs and other pests. Sometimes, the potato bugs were so thick they collected them in buckets and incinerated the insects at day's end. Blanche, too, "hated the chore of picking off potato bugs." When the potato crop matured, the Driscoll brothers had to dig up the tubers, clean them, and store them in the cellar. During the cold months, they worked in the root cellar, cutting eyes from the potatoes for seeding for the spring plantings.

Once the garden crops matured in the middle of the summer, families picked and ate the fruits—or in this case, the veggies—of their labor. Harvesting brought new chores. True to their Germanic heritage, the seven Mayer children in Dakota Territory helped make sauerkraut by stomping down cabbage in barrels of vinegar and salt water for countless hours. Blanche enjoyed picking peas and beans from the vine, an easier task than harvesting potatoes. Peas and beans, though, had to be shelled for cooking or canning. Other vegetables had to be pickled or preserved for winter use, all creating additional work, primarily for the mothers and the daughters. Some of the annual crop of beans and peas was put aside to dry out for seed to plant the next spring's garden.

Corn was a staple of both the garden and the field, as it could feed humans or livestock. When corn matured, it could be pulled by hand when the husks were still green. Once husked and cleaned of the silks, the flaxen threads that protect the kernels as they grow, corn could be boiled or roasted over a fire for meals. The kernels could also be cut from the cob and baked in a multitude of recipes. The cobs could be fed to hogs or, once they dried, used for toilet paper.

Field corn was often left on the stalk until the plant had yellowed and died. Once the kernels had dried out, the ears would be picked and husked. Then the dried kernels would be separated from the cobs and stored. Some might be sold or bartered for goods the family could not produce on their farm. Other dried corn was stored in sacks or kegs for later family use. Quantities of corn in the husk were kept in a corn crib to provide fodder for livestock during the winter months. The best ears of corn were dried and saved as seed corn for the next year's crop. Other corn would be ground into cornmeal, one of staples of the frontier diet because of its varied uses. Children helped in each step of the process.

Harvesting wheat provided a tougher challenge, especially in the early years on the plains before mechanization arrived. Because of the dangers of handling a sharp sickle or a honed scythe, men handled the chore of cutting the wheat stalks at the ground level. The stalks included the stem itself and the head, which held the seeds or grain inside a dry husk. Once removed from the grain, the hull was called chaff.

Once the men had cut the stalks of wheat, the women and children tied the plants in bundles for easier handling and then transported them to the barn or other location where they would be threshed. Before she was old enough to bind grain stalks, Matilda Peitzke helped "carry bundles in piles, ready to be shocked up" for processing. The bundles were placed on a canvas tarp where the men beat the heads of the plants with flailing tools designed to separate the head and grain from the stem and loosen the seeds from the husks. This process was called threshing.

Next, the grain and husks were separated by tossing them in special trays that caught the heavier seeds while allowing the lighter chaff and debris to be carried off by gentle air currents. This was called winnowing. Another winnowing method was to place a sheet beneath a platform on a breezy day and then dump a bucket filled with grain and husks from several feet above the cloth. This allowed the chaff to blow away while the grain fell onto the cloth.

The headless stalks of the wheat plants were saved as they could be used as straw in barns, filler in mattresses and even fuel for fires when nothing else was available. Once the grain had been separated, it could then be ground into flour for kitchen use. A benefit to children from their work was that they could chew a handful of seed, which would produce a sticky substance that substituted for gum. This helped keep their mouths moist during the dusty process of threshing and winnowing.

Even when mechanization took over the more tedious parts of the process, children still contributed to the work. Boys scoured the fields in front of the machinery to remove stones and other field debris that might damage the equipment. As threshing equipment also required more men to operate, the women and their daughters often had to provide meals for the work crew.

North Dakota lass Stephanie Prepiora recalled the hours of labor involved in feeding the workers. "When the family bought a threshing machine, my sister and I worked in the cook car—hours from four a.m. till ten p.m.—if you finished. It meant three large meals and two substantial lunches—the lunches consisted of meat sandwiches and a sweet as cake or doughnuts. We baked bread, cakes, pies, and cookies daily, and did the wash; we dug potatoes, carrots for meals; picked peas, tomatoes and all the vegetables used for meals; brought in wood for the stove and all water used. Threshing would go on for many days and sometimes if a rainy spell came, it could last for many weeks."

Pioneer farmers had to maximize the use of limited resources and the interplay between the field and livestock. In the 1870s young Bessie Felton Wilson and her brother, Bernard, at their father's direction, managed their swine one summer. "When my father had a bunch of twenty-five or thirty shoats and no corn to feed them, my brother and I herded them around over the farm wherever there was anything to be found that a hog could eat. After wheat harvest, we herded them in the stubble field. How tired we were sometimes and how sore the stubble made our feet! We had several of the hogs named, and I used to make my brother believe that they were talking when they grunted, and I, being able to understand their hog Latin, would interpret to him."

Despite the tedium and aching feet, Bessie and Bernard managed the job so well that once the swine went to market, their father used some of the profits to buy each a mail-order saddle from Montgomery Ward & Co.

Overseeing the livestock was an important chore often assigned to children, who watched them graze or took them to water. North Dakota girl Stephanie Prepiora recalled the task. "What a bore waiting for a cow to fill its enormous stomach; even the dog, who came with me, would get bored and run home."

Twelve-year-old Iowan Mary Rebecca Williams and her nine-year-old brother tended the family cattle after school each day. Remembered Mary Rebecca, we would "about four in the evening run home, and if you were passing about that time you would see a little boy and a girl with spy glass in hand mounting the house top [to] look over the prairie's to see which way the cows were." Once they spotted the livestock, they would climb down the ladder and head out after them and "return about sundown with a drove of cattle."

David Siceloff of Oklahoma's Cherokee Strip said, "Our cows were always herded on the unfenced prairie, and it was our job to see that they did not get into the crops." One day he and his brother drove their cattle near a stream bank to graze, but the boys got interested in a cave in the creek embankment and neglected the animals. The livestock strayed into a neighbor's corn patch before the boys could stop them.

After they got them out of the corn and started home, their neighbor rode up and said he was claiming the cattle since they had been on his property and eaten portions of his crop. To emphasize his point, the fellow drew his pistol and aimed it at the siblings.

Eight-year-old David shook his head and called to his brother. "Come on. Let's take our cows home. He's not going to shoot us. If he does, they'll hang him from his own tree." Years later, Siceloff looked back on the incident. "Pretty tall talk for an eight-year-old, I would say. I wonder where I got it? The answer is that I was raised on it. It was a rough country."

In Dakota Territory the seven children of the Mayer family had to herd cattle until each turned twenty-one or left home. In those days, the lack of fences and limited visibility made the job difficult, as grasses often grew taller than young children. While the tall grasses were an impediment to children tending livestock, they also provided a resource that pioneers used to feed their animals. Parents and children would cut or mow the tall grass, then bundle or bale it to keep in the hay shed to provide fodder for animals during the sparse winter months.

With the harvesting cycle in the fall came the certainty winter was approaching, and the family hastened their efforts to prepare for the impending cold.

In the fall, Siceloff recalled, "We knew that winter was coming, and that meant summer followed upon its heels, and provisions for both must be made. We chopped wood, harvested whatever crops had been left to us, and dried and canned peaches and apples until I was sick of the sight of them. A barrel sauerkraut was prepared, hogs butchered, sausage made, lard rendered, and hams and bacon smoked."

The chores never ceased in Siceloff's mind. "There were so many things for a young settler to learn…. I waited and listened and went about routine affairs. They were not very exciting. I watered the garden, milked the cows, picketed cows, hung milk in the well [to cool], churned, and ran errands. There were so many things that had to be done that I could not keep track of them."

The childhood work never ended, it just changed as children got older, stronger and smarter.

North Dakota girl Stephanie Prepiora remembered, "As we grew older, more work was required of us, as [it] was of all farm children. We milked the cows, helped clean the barn and chicken coop, fed animals and poultry, baled and stacked hay, shocked grain, helped with the plowing, helped with the housework and cooking."

As an adult, author Hamlin Garland summed up his experience as a juvenile worker on the prairies. "A boy wants to do everything, but he doesn't want to do anything long. No matter how enjoyable a job may be for a time, it soon grows old to him. He is an experimenter. That is his trade. To do one thing long cuts him off from acquiring a complete education. Moreover, he wants to do a man's work. Set him to turning bundles, he longs to pitch in the field, or some other job for which he is not fitted."

More often than not, pintsized pioneers did their chores, whether or not they were fitted for them. It was the way it had to be for many families to survive.

Chapter Six

# Cows and Boys

On a brisk January 1885 night in New York City, eleven-year-old Fred Shephard, the son of a prosperous banker, broke into his piggy bank, gathered what belongings he thought he would need and climbed down the rainspout to the Manhattan street below.

An avid reader of Western dime novels, young Shephard ran away from home that night to fulfill his ambition. Fred disappeared without a trace, the only clue to his intent turned up at his school in his latest dime novel. Across the bottom of the opening page of the book, he penciled in his plans. "Ime (sic) goin' West to be a cowboy detective."

His father hired detectives to search for Fred, and although they investigated leads as far away from Manhattan as Wyoming and Arizona, the youngster never turned up. Whether he fulfilled his dream or met a tragic end remains a mystery, but young Fred, like many peers of his era, found a glamor in ranching or investigative work. They didn't share such excitement about farming, and there's no known record of an adolescent male running away from home to become a sod-buster detective, though many farm boys did abandon the plow for the lariat.

As a young man, Kentuckian Edgar Rye moved to west Texas in the early 1870s and observed the rise of the cowboy. The sometime journalist Rye would years later describe in romantic terms the cow herders, which is what they were and often what they were called at the time. “To see the cowboy in all his glory, one must catch a glimpse of him on horseback as he gallops over the prairie. In the saddle he is at home, and the more spirited the horse, the better pleased the rider. The horse and rider seem one, like the centaur, so much in harmony are their motions. The broad-brimmed hat, leather leggings, and six-shooter go to make up the uniform that distinguishes him from the rest of the world.”

Riding a steed across the plains appealed to youthful imaginations much more than following a mule and plow day after day over a quarter section of land. Ranch work and herding cattle were no less strenuous chores than farm duties, often more so. It was also more dangerous, especially on trail drives. That, too, may have been part of its appeal to city boys and farm kids as it fulfilled their dreams of adventure.

Iowa farm boy Walker D. Wyman said the joy of watching livestock grow on the farm “could not compete with the excitement of digging for gold in the Rockies or trailing a herd from Texas to Montana. The Black Hills was a center of wild tales during my boyhood, and when I was ten, three of us young bloods started to go there, but gave it up after walking fifteen or twenty miles one hot day." When he turned twenty-two, Wyman fulfilled his boyhood dream and headed west to become a cowhand.

Other frontier kids didn't wait that long to quit following the family plow or their parents' instructions. Instead, they ran away to work cattle. Barely ten years old, Henry Young of Coryell County, Texas, abandoned his home when he "wasn't bigger than a pint of cider." As he described it, "One night I filled a fifty-pound flour sack half full of chuck and some clothes, sneaked a hoss out of the pen, put a pigskin saddle on it, and rode away, headed northwest."

Certain his father would track him down and force him back home, young Henry traveled only at night and slept during the day far from the roads. He claimed he saw not a single person for two hundred miles until he arrived in Colorado City, Texas, and asked for work. A liveryman suggested he try the CA Bar ranch several miles outside of town.

He found the stone house that was the ranch headquarters and hollered his presence. The woman of the place greeted him and asked him what he needed. "Is the boss man at home?" Young answered. She replied not yet, but he soon would be for supper, if he cared to wait. She asked about his business, and he replied he was looking for work. Though she asked his name, he refused to tell her, finally admitting he had run away from home and didn't want his folks to find him.

When rancher Bill Adair arrived for supper, he and Young joined his wife at the kitchen table where the famished Young ate with abandon. "That was the best-looking chuck, and the best-tasting, that I ever stuffed into my mouth. When I finished, Adair said, 'You can handle chuck all right.'" Adair acknowledged that Young ate his supper with abandon, a sign the boy must be a hard worker. He agreed to give Henry a job, provided he divulge his name. The ten-year-old still refused.

"I have to call you [something]; can't just say 'Here, fellow,'" Adair informed him, but Young kept his secret. "Kid," Adair said, "you have plenty sand in your gizzard." Then Adair named him "Half Pint Emerson," a name Young carried for four years. Adair outfitted Henry in work clothes, boots, Stetson, spurs, and bandana, which he debited from Young's twenty-five-dollar-a-month pay. At ten years old, Half Pint was a cowboy, just as he had dreamed.

After a year of training in the ways of cattle and the cowboy, the rancher turned Half Pint loose and at eleven years old he was doing a cowhand's regular chores of "line riding, night or day and all other work" on sixty square miles of west Texas ranch land that supported almost 10,000 cattle. Half Pint worked for four years at cowboying for Adair in Texas and New Mexico before returning to his Coryell County home on the same horse he had departed on. He approached the house near dusk. When his mother came to the door, he asked if he could stay the night.

Not recognizing her own son, she said he could and invited him inside, welcoming him to sit by the fireplace while she lit a coal-oil lamp on the mantle. "What may your name be, stranger?" she asked.

"They call me Half Pint Emerson," Henry replied.

"Where you all from?"

"From the West," he answered.

"I have a boy. Henry Young is his name. He left here four years ago, and we have not heard hide or hair from him since. By chance, you may have met up with Henry?"

As the lamp illuminated the room, she gasped. "Are you Henry?"

Remembered Young years later, "I began to smile, and at the same time tears crowded my eyes and the corners of my mouth began to quiver. Before I could say a word, she said, 'God has blessed me. It's my boy.'"

Though he expected a thrashing or a tongue-lashing when his father came home, Henry "Half Pint Emerson" Young received a glad welcome instead. His dad "acted sort of proud of me." Henry Young would stay in the cattle business for the rest of his career.

Other boys—and even girls—started early working longhorns, some on family ranches and others for larger outfits all across the West. Those pintsized pioneers worked herds, delivered supplies to line camps, built corrals and fences, and carried responsibilities well beyond their youthful years.

In 1869 Hiram G. Craig of Bellville, Texas, deserted home at fourteen. As he explained it, "Father was the proud possessor of a small bunch of cattle, and created a desire in me to be a cowboy—to have a good horse, saddle, leggings, spurs and to handle cattle … I ran away from home and went to work for … one of the biggest ranch owners of that time. I was proud of my job, which, however, was of short duration. My brother learned of my whereabouts and came and took me home. I remained at home with my parents for three years, when the call of the 'wild' again overcame me."

At fifteen south Texas youth E.L. Brounson helped drive a thousand head of longhorns in 1883 to Goliad County to escape the drought that threatened their herd back home.

Though she had brothers, Lily Klasner in New Mexico Territory wound up handling a lot of livestock chores by necessity. "Business required that Father be away much of the time. Because I was the strongest and healthiest of the children, it became my obligation to do much of the riding and caring for cattle that ordinarily would have evolved upon my older brothers. Neither failed to do all he could, but I realized in later years that it was I upon whom my parents depended. I did not resent that, but was proud of my ability to ride, rope, brand, and perform the various functions of a cowboy."

C.W. Ackerman of Bexar County, Texas, remembered, "When I was a boy, rounding up cattle was a very exciting event. In those days people did not have their pastures fenced, so the cattle often wandered many miles from home." Young C.W. went on his first cow hunt at age six. Accompanying his ten-year-old brother, the pintsized Ackerman found a mother and calf, which his older brother instructed him to guard while he searched for other livestock. After his brother departed, little C.W. lost the two animals in the high grass and brush and started after them. He failed to find the animals, and his brother couldn't find him, returning home to report C.W. missing.

Before C.W. stumbled upon the home of a sympathetic Mexican family, he had traveled twenty miles from his place in search of the mother and calf. The little boy spent two nights without food or cover, endured a violent thunderstorm, and even spent part of the time in a tree for safety from howling wolves. The compassionate Mexican man fed C.W. and loaded the boy on his donkey, returning him to the Ackerman household, where the lost boy's father gave a nice reward to his son's savior.

"I was just fourteen years old when I went out on my first roundup," C.W. remembered. "My father put me in the care of our captain (foreman) and from him I learned how to rope and brand cattle and many other important things one should know about roundups."

"I often roped and branded as many as eight or ten calves by myself in a day," C.W. recalled. "Branding was not a very easy task, either, for we had to run the brand. We had no ready-made brands as now. Many times we had to gather the wilder cattle at night. When they went out on the prairie, we would build a stockade around water holes, leaving only one opening for the cattle to get in. Even with such a trap, we were often unable to hold the wildest ones in." He made his first drive to Kansas in 1873, "when I was a boy of eighteen."

Missouri native M.A. Withers, who moved with his family to Caldwell County, Texas, when he was six, went on his initial cattle drive at thirteen from Lockhart to Fredericksburg, Texas, a distance of one hundred and twenty miles. Three years later in 1862, he made a three-hundred-and-thirty-mile drive to Shreveport, Louisiana, to sell beef to the Confederacy to feed Southern soldiers. After serving in the Confederate Army, he averaged a cattle drive a year between 1868 and 1887. "I had a number of flattering offers to remain in the North in the cattle business, but I loved Texas so well that I always returned after each drive."

At sixteen in 1882, Jack Potter of San Antonio left home on a trail excursion that would take him from south Texas to central Montana. "There was no excitement whatever on this drive," Jack said of his thirty-dollar-a-month job. The trip home, though, was a different matter for this naïve cowhand, as railroad and travel protocols confounded him.

"Here I was, a boy not yet seventeen years old, two thousand miles from home. I had never been on a railroad train, had never slept in a hotel, never taken a bath in a bath house, and from babyhood I had heard terrible stories about ticket thieves, moneychangers, pickpockets, three-card monte, and other robbing schemes, and I had horrors about this, my first railroad trip." After his trail boss secured him a ticket, he bought a trunk to pack his saddle and belongings for the return to San Antonio.

From Montana through Dodge City and back to San Antonio, Jack rode bewildered by connections to new trains which seemed to be headed in the wrong direction. He was confused because after he checked his trunk, railway employees took it from him and loaded it for him. Jack wouldn't see his baggage for days. His first rail ride home was in his memory more perplexing and dangerous than the trail drive which had ended so far from Texas.

At nine years old, George W. Brock of Caldwell County, Texas, "commenced to handle stock, but at that time I was too small to get on a horse unaided, and my father told me not to get off, but every time I saw a rabbit I would get off and throw rocks at it, and then I would have to be helped back on my horse." Two years later George went on his first herding trip with his father in 1871.

At sixteen Bastrop resident Ben Drake in 1871 finally convinced his mother to let him accompany a friend on a trail drive up north. His pal had promised the company would outfit him, which it did, providing Ben first with a pair of fourteen-dollar custom-made boots. Ben also received a pair of bell spurs, a Colt six-shooter, a rim-fire Winchester carbine, and a pair of twelve-dollar leggings. "This was the first time in my life," Ben recalled, "that I had been rigged out, and you bet I was proud." After he bought horses and saddle gear on credit, he was ready for his first trail drive.

Ben, his pal, and a herd of 2,500 headed out in March 1871 for Kansas City, arriving weeks later after a grueling but enlightening trip. The trail hands returned to Austin, where they received their wages. After settling debts for the horses and equipment, Ben returned to the family homestead. "When I reached home, I gave all of my wages to my mother, stayed there three days and went back to the ranch to work."

Born in 1856, H.C. Williams grew up on a stock farm in Refugio County, Texas, and at age fifteen built seven miles of barbed wire fence, the first in San Patricio County, for a pair of area ranchers.

E.M. "Bud" Daggett, a Shelby County, Texas, native, loved the ranching community, an affection that began in his childhood. "I went into the saddle at ten years old. The first night I can remember of camping out on a cow hunt was in the spring of that year. We camped on the banks of a creek called Deer Creek, south of Fort Worth about fifteen miles. At that time the boys carried their biscuits and dried beef and a little coffee in sacks tied behind their saddles, and their blankets generally piled on their saddle blankets and their saddles on top of that making a packhorse out of the boys' saddle ponies. From that time on, I have worked with cattle a part of every year without missing a single year for over sixty years and am still handling cattle as a commission man and salesman on the stockyards."

When Marvin Powe was nine years old, his ranchman father sent him out to find and return some horses that had wandered off. Young Marvin took his job seriously, searching one, two, three and then four days without success and tracking the horses well beyond ranch property. Not caring to disappoint his father, he kept at it, living off the land and camping with occasional cowboys as he pursued his quest. A week after he began his search, Marvin found the horses and returned them to the ranch. His father had expected no less from his son and had expressed only slight concern over his son's lengthy absence. Marvin persevered, as his father knew he would because of the lessons of work and responsibility instilled in him.

Richard C. Phillips began riding when he was four years old on his father's XX Ranch outside Bandera, Texas. It was a good thing because his father died "just after I'd learned to ride pretty good and could climb up by myself. After he died, that left nobody but me and my mother, so I had to learn to tend to the hundred-odd head of stuff we had."

His mother would "talk to me and try to make me feel my responsibility so's I'd go out there and do my dead level best to take my dad's place. I'd never have made it, though, if it hadn't been for the good neighbors we all had around there. They done a marvelous lot for us and took the load in the roundups."

Richard remembered, "I went on the roundups, all right, and slept out away from home during them roundups. Come branding time, and I was right in the middle of it, tending to the irons and everything else a stripling could shake. One thing about it, though, and that was there wasn't a lazy bone in my body, and I learnt to rope and brand on my own account. I reckon I could pull it all off by the time I was eight years old. That's pretty young, but in them days a kid wasn't always hanging out in some ice cream parlor. Instead, he went about his business and tried to be some account in the world."

When he was just twelve, young Richard's mother died, leaving him an orphan or "dogie," which is what cowboys called a motherless calf. Though he never learned to read, which accounts for the mistakes in his grammar, he could support himself the rest of his life in the livestock trade.

Bill Dobbs, a Fannin County Texan, “rode horses when I was too little even to climb up by the stirrups, but had to have some cowpoke to give me a boost so I could get into the saddle.” Of his youthful ranch experiences, he remembered, “between five and twelve, I was taught to work cattle just like the rest of the waddies on the place.... My first stay away from home was when I was about twelve, or maybe a little less. I stayed out on the regular roundup for three months. You know, where there’s a lot of cattle on the ranch, the critters will drift. We’d have to go into four and five counties to round up the Muleshoe [Ranch] stock all around the ranch and on other ranches. In that roundup, I slept just like the regular hands. Used my saddle for a pillow and my saddle blanket for a mattress.”

At age six, Troy B. Cowan went on a hundred-and-ninety-mile drive from Anderson to Erath counties in Texas, herding 1,500 three- and four-year-old steers. His father “took on some cowpokes, and we started west with the herd. Of course, I didn’t do any night riding or roping. The only thing I done on the drive was to hustle the stragglers and help keep the herd together. That’s an important thing on any cattle drive and keeps the cowpokes busy doing it.” By the time he was thirteen, Troy rode night herd with the rest of the cowboys and roped and handled all their normal chores.

On the family's later drives, Troy's "sisters rode and roped with us and did all of the cooking, so they really didn't take as big a hand as they could have if they'd been allowed away from the cooking end of things." His sisters weren't the only girls he saw doing cattle work.

Troy noted, "There were a couple of cowgirls on the Lazy S spread that could really ride and rope better than any women ever I seen. Their names were Ethel and Bess Andres. They were what I'd call boys in girls' clothing because they sure took the place of a boy on the range. I'm not talking from hearsay; I'm talking from seeing them do it. Why, I've seen them riding after a cow critter and come to a place where they had to do some fancy riding, and you could see light between them and the saddle."

Illinois native H.P. Cook went up the trail from Decatur, Texas, to Fort Dodge, Kansas, in 1871 with several thousand head of cattle, twelve cowboys and a chuck wagon. He had just celebrated his tenth birthday. "I made a regular hand on the trail, too, and took my place on the shifts at night after the cattle were bedded down. You know, back in those days, lots of boys were good cowboys by the time they were ten years old."

Though he didn't work cattle on a large ranch, nine-year-old Cliff Newland in west Texas hauled supplies to area line camps to provide provisions for cowhands working away from their ranch headquarters. Newland's task meant a regular round trip of seventy-five miles, for which he earned fifty cents a day to help support his widowed father and himself on their small spread.

On remote ranches, children often served as the e-mail of the day. Young New Mexico girl Agnes Morley described it this way: "'Put-a-kid-on-a-horse' was the formula for sending messages. Between our several ranch establishments messages had to go back and forth continually; and we children carried them. Sometimes we led a packhorse loaded with supplies, or if the size of the load did not justify an extra horse, our own saddles were hung with bulging sacks until we resembled juvenile mounted Santa Clauses."

Once when her father got word that a steer-buyer in Magdalena some fifty miles distant from their ranch was offering the top prices of the season, he sent Agnes to find the ranch foreman with instructions to inform the buyer of the number of cattle he would provide and the date of delivery. Her brother Ray, who Agnes described as "still a very small boy," was working with other ranch hands rounding up the cattle. The foreman assigned Ray to deliver the message to the cattle buyer before he left on the train in a couple of days.

Young Ray took the missive and the best horse, riding for Magdalena with the transaction details. Undeterred even by a mother grizzly bear and her two cubs that delayed his trek by hours, Ray made it to Magdalena in time to catch the man and deliver the message that increased ranch profits that year. In all, the small boy rode more than a hundred miles alone to close the deal.

Years after he had taken up the cow business as a young man, Wyman D. Walker looked back over his life with this assessment: "I have done a lot of bad things in my life, but I never did stoop to sheep ranching." While Wyman displayed a common attitude of cattlemen against sheepherders, sheep became a valuable, if not glamorous, option for many western families who put their children to work tending the flocks.

After visiting Edward Farrell, a prosperous sheep raiser headquartered twenty miles west of Laramie, Wyoming, a correspondent for *The American Agriculturist* in 1879, headed west and the next day came upon an isolated sheep camp with a corral and rude dugout twelve miles from Farrell's home. The magazine reporter relished the fact the two sheepherders were Farrell's own sons, who were managing a flock of 2,300 sheep. Wrote the journalist, "There was a good range here, and the father had in spring time sent the sheep and the boys to possess it … You will be surprised when I tell you that these lads, entrusted with the care of over 2,000 sheep, and living here in this remote, secluded spot, were only eleven and thirteen years of age."

The correspondent reported that the two boys shot their game, did their cooking and "lived entirely alone with their dogs and two ponies employed in herding the sheep." The two pintsized pioneers alternated watch over the sheep, protecting them from bears, wolves, and other wild animals. Concluded the journalist, "It is astonishing, the early self-reliance which these frontier children display, and the skill which, as mere urchins, they attain in herding sheep."

Pintsized sheepherder Ralla Banta in west Texas enjoyed her task of keeping watch over the sheep and moving them from place to place for grazing. "When we returned home in the evening, we enjoyed telling where we had been, to what creek, up what branch and what we had seen." An 1880s visitor to northern Nebraska reported, "It has been a novel sight to watch a little girl about ten years old herding sheep..., handling her pony with a masterly hand, galloping around the flock if they begin to scatter out, and driving them into a corral."

Young Nebraskan Frank Dean never grew accustomed to the solitude of herding sheep. "I think the most lonesome time I had was when I herded sheep.... I was eleven years old, and to be out all day seeing nothing but prairie and sheep was enough to make a boy lonesome."

Dean may have been lonely, but he was not alone as countless other youth looked after sheep across the frontier, including dozens listed in the 1880 Federal Census in Kansas. Some of those Kansas herders were as young as eight years old. Those eight-year-olds included Charles Reagan and Hiram Smith in Sumner County and John P. Rosener in Edwards County, among others. Even though many westerners herded sheep, the task earned no glamor in the dime novels, magazines, or newspapers of the time. Consequently, accounts of sheep herding are not nearly as numerous as those of herding cattle. Herding sheep was a chore. Herding longhorns, by contrast, was an adventure.

Of all the young trail hands Texan Samuel Dunn Houston hired in his years in the cattle business, none could match Willie Matthews. Needing additional help as he neared Clayton, New Mexico, he went to town looking for men to put on the payroll. Finding none, he heard of a "kid" that was interested in riding the trail. He found the youth named Willie Matthews, who claimed to be nineteen years old, but looked younger than that with his soft features and his frail hundred-and-twenty-pound body. Despite Matthew's puny frame, the skeptical Houston put the youth to work.

"I was so pleased with him that I wished many times that I could find two or three more like him," Houston recalled of young Willie. "The kid would get up the darkest stormy nights and stay with the cattle until the storm was over. He was good natured, very modest, didn't use any cuss words or tobacco, and was always pleasant."

Willie remained a stellar employee for three months until the herd reached Hugo, Colorado, a railroad stop near the Colorado-Wyoming border. As the cattle were bedding down and supper was ending, Willie told Houston he was homesick and wanted to return home to Caldwell, Kansas. Though the trail boss hated to lose such a fine hand, Houston accepted Willie's resignation, and sent the cowhand on his way to Hugo.

Toward sundown, Houston and his men saw an attractive young woman approaching their camp. "I couldn't imagine why a woman would be coming on foot to a cow camp, but she kept right on coming and when within fifty feet of camp, I got up to be ready to receive my guest. Our eyes were all set on her, and every man holding his breath. When she got up within about twenty feet of me, she began to laugh, and said, 'Mr. Houston, you don't know me, do you?'"

Houston stood speechless for a minute, not believing his eyes. Finally, he spoke. "Kid, is it possible that you are a lady?" Indeed it was! Willie Matthews was a girl!

"We were so dumbfounded, we could hardly think of a thing to say. I told the cook to get one of the tomato boxes for a chair. The kid sat down, and I said, 'Now I want you to explain yourself.'"

Miss Matthews, perhaps named Wilma though her exact given name has disappeared from history, explained that her father had been "an old-time trail driver" from south Texas. In the 1870s, he drove a herd from southern Texas to Caldwell and liked the Kansas rangeland so much that he started ranching there. He married and had a daughter, who at ten years old grew fascinated with her papa's talk about life on the cow trail.

"I made up my mind," Miss Matthews informed her cow outfit, "that when I was grown up, I was going up the trail if I had to run off." And she did just that, abandoning home to reach Clayton, where several herds were rumored to be passing. In New Mexico, she put on boy's clothing and joined up with Houston's outfit. "Now, Mr. Houston," she continued, "I am glad I found you to make the trip with, for I have enjoyed it. I am going just as straight home as I can, and that old train can't run too fast for me when I get on it."

Houston picked up the story from there. "The train left Hugo at 11:20 o'clock in the evening. I left one man with the herd and took the kid and every man to town to see the little girl off. I suppose she was the only girl that ever made such a trip as that. She was a perfect lady." And, a perfect cow hand!

Such was the romance and appeal of the cowboy life—even if it was hard and dirty work—that it could cause a New York City boy like Fred Shepard or a Kansas girl like "Wilma" Matthews to run away from home to experience it.

Chapter Seven

# Towns and Tykes

Though she lived on a ranch, young Agnes Morley took a twenty-mile round trip to town once a week to collect the family mail. Sometimes she made the journey alone and at other times with her younger brother, Ray, down Datil Canyon to the nearest post office in northern New Mexico Territory.

"With icicles six inches long hanging from my pony's nostrils, and with frostbitten feet, I have made the trip in sub-zero weather or, in midsummer; I have ridden it with the sun blasting down with all the force of a glass furnace," Agnes remembered years later.

Challenging though the conditions may have been on the outing, the weekly chore gave Agnes the chance to reach civilization. Even a small community offered more excitement for a young girl or boy than the isolation of ranch life. And since her parents subscribed to several magazines and newspapers, the mail broadened her horizons beyond that of the New Mexico landscape.

Kansan Blanche Beale remembered, "Town people had chores to do much like country people. For behind every house in our neighborhood, there was a barn and a chicken house, fruit trees, and a big garden."

Like their country cousins, city children still did many of the same chores that farm and ranch kids handled. Town tykes milked cows, tended gardens, gathered and cut firewood, tended their horses, and toted water, among other tasks. Often these pintsized pioneers also assisted their mothers and fathers in their various town occupations.

As certain as Agnes Morley was of her weekly mail run, young Kansan Della Knowles knew she would go to the post office regularly as well. Della helped her father, who was postmaster of their local community. Besides her regular household chores, Della spent a lot of time at the post office helping her dad sort and distribute the letters, magazines, and parcels.

The difference between rural and town residents was that children in settlements had more varied work possibilities, depending upon the occupations of their parents. For example, Kansas brothers Edward and Will Beck worked as printer's devils, setting type for their father in his print shop. Town kids helped in general stores, stables, hotels, restaurants, clothing stores, meat markets, bathhouses, millinery shops, banks, drugstores, boot stores, dry goods shops, telegraph offices, newspapers, and in whatever other environments their parents earned a living.

By the late 1890s, debates occurred in the newspapers and among folks over whether the farm boy or the town boy was best fit for life. The *Des Moines Homestead*—its name betraying its stance on the issue—stated "in the race of life, the farm boy leads the town boy." To begin with, the *Homestead* argued "that the farm offers to the boy a systematic physical development," as well as the opportunity to learn from nature and the outdoors, rather than being confined "in badly ventilated apartments." Too, the *Homestead* suggested the farm made boys better financial managers since they had so "few opportunities to spend money" whereas "the town boy … enters in the struggle for life with habits of expenditure far beyond his personal means of gratification."

Further, the *Homestead* believed the farm provided chores of increasing responsibility to agrarian children, unlike the offspring of "the physician, the lawyer [and] the businessman." In those cases, the town boy "can do little at best in one case in a thousand to aid his father in his work."

The views of the *Homestead* represented rural concerns over more and more farm families leaving rural areas for towns and cities. A single fifteen-year-old Kansas youth, though, quickly disproved the publication's contention that town kids were of little help to their parents' professions. Lawrence Adams worked as a "nurse" during surgeries conducted by his physician father and another local doctor in their Kansas community during pioneering times.

Many small communities spawned one or more newspapers, but they all operated on a shoestring. In tiny towns, the owner often handled all office chores as he could not afford to hire additional employees. An 1830 Texas newspaper editor delineated his responsibilities. A country editor "is one who reads newspapers, selects miscellany, writes articles on all subjects; sets type, reads proof, works at press, folds papers, and sometimes carries them; prints jobs, runs on errands; cuts wood; totes water; talks to all his patrons who call; patiently receives blame for things that never were nor can be done; [and] gets little money…."

As a result, newspaper editors with children would assign them tasks like sweeping the floors or keeping the print shop tidy. As the children grew and learned to read, they took on additional responsibilities, including setting type by hand a single letter at a time and later operating a hand press. They delivered messages and carried papers to subscribers. At fourteen Sam Clemens of Hannibal, Missouri, apprenticed at a paper. After two years, when his brother Orion established a newspaper, young Sam joined him. At sixteen, in his brother's absence, Sam edited the paper himself. That experience in the printing trade and in writing and editing articles served Sam well when he began penning novels under the penname of Mark Twain.

At age eleven J. Marvin Hunter went to work in his father's newly purchased newspaper in Menardville, Texas. Later, when he started his own newspaper, the *Kimble County Crony*, he remembered the challenge of providing the news and supporting his family. "I hustled early and late for advertising patronage and subscriptions. I would trade advertising space in my paper and subscriptions to it for anything we could consume, butter, eggs, chickens, produce of any kind, and for dry goods and groceries, for I believe strictly in the system of barter and trade." As cash was scarce, Hunter had no choice but to believe in barter. By the time his newspaper reached its peak, Hunter decided, "I was like a frog in a well, going round and round, and getting nowhere."

Another Texan who began newspapering in his youth was sixteen-year-old Don Hampton Biggers, who learned to set type, to operate a printing press and to report news at the *Colorado City Clipper* in west Texas. Those skills learned in his younger years served Biggers well as he made journalism his life's career. In later life both Biggers and Hunter would use the newspaper skills of their youth to document the Texas frontier with Hunter starting the *Frontier Times* magazine and with Biggers writing a variety of books on the region's history.

Fourteen-year-old Lee Travis and fifteen-year-old James Sanders in 1875 established the *News Letter*, a weekly newspaper that covered three sprawling Montana counties. The young journalists traveled by buckboard across their circulation area to solicit subscriptions and to gather news.

By that same age, boys elsewhere across the West were taking on demanding and risky jobs such as driving a stagecoach through hostile Indian country in Arizona or navigating a ferry back and forth across an unpredictable Montana river.

After the Civil War, fourteen-year-old Prussian immigrant Frederick A. Piper, who had arrived in

Texas in 1851, initiated a vendor's route from his Victoria home to remote Uvalde County, Texas. Each trip he drove a wagon of store goods and samples from Victoria through San Antonio to Uvalde, some two hundred miles distant. Young Piper traveled alone through lands still threatened by Indians and outlaws to reach isolated families and merchants desperate for goods and supplies.

By himself Piper managed the wagon and team, keeping the animals fed and watered. On the journey west, he protected his load of merchandise from inclement weather and thieves. On the return trip, he safeguarded the proceeds of his sales from robbers. Arriving back home, he repaid the Victoria merchants their due and tallied a nice profit for himself.

In addition to learning self-reliance on his many westward trips, Piper also earned the respect of his distant customers, who viewed him as an honest and dependable worker. Along the way, he learned about the Texas landscape and identified business opportunities that intrigued him. By the time he gave up the freighting, he had secured the nest egg and reputation that allowed him to buy land and succeed as a rancher before he moved into banking and insurance with equal success.

Piper succeeded in each business endeavor as an adult and by the time he died in San Antonio at age eighty, his integrity, his work ethic, and his collegiality were universally respected among all who knew him. He attributed his accomplishments to the lessons he learned as a young freighter on dangerous Texas roads and trails.

At the age of twelve, Bennett E. Seymour began clerking for a grocer in the mining camp that became Leadville, Colorado. Within a matter of months, Ben took charge of the store whenever his boss traveled out of town. By the time he was thirteen, the youth was so trusted that his boss assigned him to pick up and deliver supplies by wagon from South Park, Colorado, a round trip of a hundred miles. The clerking skills he learned early on and the dependability he displayed in his work propelled him to establish the Hawley Mercantile Company as an adult. Consequently, he became a prominent Colorado merchant and financier after the turn of the twentieth century.

As a young girl following her mother to various Colorado mining camps after her father deserted the family, Anne Ellis helped wash and iron laundry for miners. Then she would deliver the clean clothes and even collect payment. As a Montana boy, Milton Barnhart peddled his mother's home-cooked pies, selling them for a dollar apiece to locals.

Around Virginia City, Montana, Mary Ronan developed several schemes to make money. With a friend, she would visit placer mining claims each evening as the miners were ending a day's work and volunteer to clean out the workers' sluice boxes with their hair brushes. The girls not only spruced up the mining contraptions but also freed fine gold dust or tiny gold nuggets that had sifted into the cracks. Though the gold wasn't much, it still had value that the girls cashed in. Remembered young Mary, "A man would have entered another's sluice box at the risk of being shot on sight, but it amused the miners to have us little girls clean up after them." And, she might have added, pick the miners' pockets of profits in the process.

Adolescent Mary and her friends during the spring and summer also gathered lamb's quarters—a leafy vegetable with broccoli-like flowering shoots—and other edible plants and weeds from the gullies and meadows around Virginia City. She sold buckets of the vegetation for a dollar and a half apiece. Later, as the town's prosperity grew, Mary and her pals picked wildflowers, which they made into bouquets and sold to hotels and restaurants to adorn their dining room tables.

Young New Mexican Jack Stockbridge not only raised vegetables to sell, but sometimes traveled thirty miles a day, mostly afoot, peddling his produce to raise money to help him escape from an abusive older brother at home.

A common career path for both town and country girls, some as young as twelve or thirteen, was teaching. In Oklahoma's Cherokee Strip, fifteen-year-old Clara Ewell started a subscription class in her father's store. She charged fifty cents a month per pupil. While Clara did not get rich, she enriched her students by teaching them their A-B-C's and their 1-2-3's. Ada Vrooman, another Cherokee Outlet lass, began giving classroom instruction in her community at sixteen.

In the American West, two types of towns typically evolved on the frontier: agricultural communities and mining camps. The ag settlements relied on the farms and ranches, which produced crops and livestock. By contrast, mining towns depended upon miners and machinery, which extracted resources, including gold, silver, copper, and other minerals.

These two types of towns shaped the chores children undertook. The agricultural-based towns provided typical city opportunities to work for merchants and service providers. While mining towns, as they developed, offered these same tasks for children, the style of mining in a region determined other chores open to children.

Two types of mining dominated the American frontier: placer mining and lode mining. Placer mining, at its simplest, is the equivalent of panning for gold. Though after a gold strike, the pans gave way to sluice boxes, rockers, and other contraptions that would run more water and gravel through the system to find more gold quicker. Lode mining, however, required enormous sums of capital, expensive mining equipment, and dangerous explosives to burrow deep underground to find the minerals. While lode mining was deemed too hazardous for children, anyone could pan for gold, including children.

In the 1863 mining camp of Placerville, Idaho, five-year-old Emma Jane Davison with her two- and seven-year-old brothers worked the creeks for gold. As Emma moved the rocker back and forth, her older brother shoveled gravel into the box while her baby brother dumped cans of water into the contraption. As Emma pistoned the rocker, the gravel sifted out while the heavier gold remained in the implement's trap. At eleven years old, pintsized pioneer F.M. McCarty shoveled gravel in a placer operation.

Like Mary Ronan, who brushed out sluice boxes to find gold fragments and dust, children in mining communities often followed miners into stores and—if they could get away with it—into saloons and pick up any precious metals they dropped during their purchases. Some children volunteered to sweep the floors of businesses so they could collect any gold dust they might brush into a dust pan. Others, like the children of Leadville, waited outside Pap Wyman's saloon and the town's other popular drinking establishments after busy Friday, Saturday, and Sunday nights. After the floors were swept into the gutters, the boys and girls would run their fingers through the debris in search of gold dust, nuggets, or coins dropped during the previous night's transactions. While their "plank-floor prospecting" seldom resulted in a large payday, it provided for some ready spending money for the kids to buy rock candy, a piece of fruit or a gift for a sibling.

While lode mining operations rarely allowed boys to go underground to work, they hired some youth for above-ground jobs. At thirteen Walter Smith started as an assistant cook for a mine in Tellurium, Colorado. Some of the veteran miners took a shine to him and invited him to go below ground, which he ultimately did. He handled sledge hammers, toted rock and mining debris to mining cars for removal, and even picked up some blacksmithing skills useful in mining. Though an exception to the rule, Smith may have been the youngest hard-rock miner in the country.

More common jobs for mining town children between the ages of six and sixteen were deliveries, peddling newspapers, feeding livestock, waiting tables, washing dishes and shoveling snow.

In the 1890s Ted Bennett grew up in the Colorado mining town of Creede with his brother Don and his mother after his father abandoned them. He handled a bundle of jobs as he matured in the state's last silver boomtown. Between the discovery of silver in 1889 and 1892, the population exploded from six hundred to more than 10,000 folks. The growth offered plenty of job possibilities, some paid and some just for fun.

By the time he was a young teen, Ted, under the supervision of muleskinners, had driven freight wagons pulled by four-horse teams up narrow and treacherous mountain roads to deliver supplies to mines. The job sounded difficult, but a well-trained team that knew the route and the routine simplified the task. "All we did, really, was to hold the lines. The horses took the wagon up the hill, and the skinners, walking in pairs, visited and threw rocks and other debris out of the road" ahead of the team.

As Ted explained it, the juvenile understudies received instructions to "always to swing wide on the switchbacks," or short curves, going up the incline. Being a boy, Ted decided it was quicker and better to take a short turn. When he pulled the reins to take a narrower turn, the lead animals balked, then finally obliged him. Meanwhile, the two trailing horses continued by instinct to go wide as they were trained to do.

"Right soon I had as pretty a jack-knife as one would want to see … so the horses, figuring, no doubt, that further progress was impossible under those conditions stopped and waited for someone to show up who knew something about driving."

While the muleskinner "patiently untangled the mess," Ted awaited the tongue-lashing he deserved and expected, but the fellow just asked, "Having a little trouble, boy?" After fixing the problem, the skinner surprised Ted by sending him on to the top of the mountain with the load. "When I thanked him for not kicking my pants off the wagon, he said, 'Why should I? We all got to learn sometimes it's best to do as we're told.'"

Years later, Bennett reflected on that incident. "As I look back on it now," he recalled, "I realize how much those muleskinners, practically all of them unmarried, did to help our parents bring up a bunch of men."

Young Ted's mom later married a muleskinner, who gave up the freighting business and worked in the mines, prospering enough to buy land to maintain a horse herd to rent mounts to locals and visitors. Keeping the horses meant building fences, and Ted and his brother Don were tasked with digging postholes for a fence a mile and a quarter long.

For a barbed wire fence, the space between posts will vary, but a good average is twelve feet apart. That meant the two brothers needed to dig a minimum of five hundred and fifty postholes. Their stepfather specified each posthole must be twenty-four inches deep to hold tight. Unfortunately, for Ted and Don, much of their land was rocky. Their stepdad "was pretty well discouraged when we came in on Saturday afternoons with a report that we had dug twenty or so holes that week." He went out to try his hand and discovered the flint rock was tough digging. With all his adult strength, it took him two hours to finish a hole two feet deep. He realized his stepsons could need as much as a whole workday to complete a single posthole.

Ted remembered "the afternoon when we ran out of the rocks, and next day we dug sixty-four holes before we ran into the next rocky ridge."

The pintsized pioneers in mining communities also had other, less taxing jobs for themselves or their families. "Mining camp kids in the nineties didn't know what an allowance was," Ted Bennett recalled. "What we got to spend we earned, mostly. And many were the ways we earned it."

For instance, Ted sometimes played cupid to earn a few cents. In mining camps, courting-age girls were scarce, and their fathers seldom welcomed the young men who wanted to court them. In some cases, the fathers even threatened to shoot on sight their daughters' unwelcomed beaus. Ted and some of his friends delivered clandestine notes between the young couples.

"Carrying notes between such a pair was hazardous employment and required some finesse in getting notes to and from the young lady without her parents catching on, so we always demanded a quarter for this service," Ted said.

Before he was sixteen, young Ted also delivered regular mail up the mountain from Creede to another mining burg named Bachelor. He made the trip six days a week, leaving Creede a half hour after the ten o'clock train arrived with the mail to distribute along his two-mile route. He returned in time for outgoing letters to be sorted for the train's four-twenty afternoon departure. Ted earned a dollar and a half a day for his efforts.

Just like on the prairie, fuel remained a prime concern in mining towns. After Ted and Don Bennett received pocket watches from their stepfather, they took inspiration from Mark Twain's *The Adventures of Tom Sawyer* to con their friends into doing the Bennett brothers' chores for them. In the novel, Tom Sawyer convinces his pals that it is an honor and fun to whitewash Aunt Polly's fence. Taken in by his smooth line, his buddies beg to be so honored and wind up finishing the task for him.

Using their watches to time each other, they put out word among their Creede buddies that no boy in town could saw logs into firewood quicker than they could. "We boasted about our watches and told that we had timed ourselves on the wood saw and knew for sure that we could saw more wood, faster, than any kid in town. In time, it took."

The two brothers arranged wood-sawing tournaments, making sure arguments ensued, requiring a "re-saw" and the cutting of more wood. "By the time the novelty had worn off and the competitive spirit had died down, several logs had become blocks without any effort on our part," Ted reported.

Some kids in other mining communities resorted to larceny or outright thievery to provide fuel. In the thriving mining district around Butte, Montana, many local boys and girls would collect coal that fell from coal cars along the railroad tracks. Sometimes their parents would even encourage them to jump on the rail cars and toss off chunks of coal. Catherine Hoy, who took part in the scheme, remembered, "The coal cars would run back and forth on Anaconda Road. One kid would get in the coal car and throw out all this coal. Then the rest of us would go along and pick it up and take it home." The hazardous scheme sometimes resulted in children being maimed or killed.

Other Butte children congregated around mine entrances to retrieve wood scraps left from the timbering process in mine shafts. They would carry the pieces home to cook their food or heat their houses in winter. Ann Skocilich and her siblings didn't have to fetch the wood, but they had to chop and cut it during the summer months for the harsh winter ahead. Remembered little Ann, "My dad would haul in this old wood from the smelter, and we would have to saw it and chop it and pile it. That was our [summer] vacation."

One summer the Bennett brothers in Creede, Colorado, managed "the town herd" made up of milk cows city folks had kept in town during the winter. With warm weather and meadows available for grazing, the boys on horseback drove the cows to feed each morning and returned them in time for their afternoon milking. For their work, they each received a dollar a month. "As a financial proposition," Ted Bennett remembered, "We just about made horse feed." In subsequent summers, the Bennett boys looked for more profitable ventures that would leave them spending money after they fed their mounts.

An advantage town kids possessed over their rural counterparts were more varied opportunities to make a buck, even if their choices were sometimes questionable. The larger the town, the more occasions for children to work. In San Francisco, for instance, female journalist Elodie Hogan chronicled some of the jobs children managed on the town's busy streets.

She started with the peddlers, including newsboys who made their sales "from sheer force of personal magnetism," though she found it unsettling if not bewildering to hear the pitches of young boys shouting about stories of "murder, war, fire, and explosions" to make their sales. The danger appalled her as newsboys dashed from the sidewalk into the middle of the street, risking a broken neck or bones, to get on and off moving cable cars in pursuit of a sale.

Hogan described the city's match boys as "a tribe of philosophers in small breeches." They sold matches. Their merchandise consisted of "four dozen bunches of matches swung over [their] shoulders in a calico bag." Even if they sold their entire stock of matches, their sales would only net them thirty-five cents. Boys as young as six sold newspapers and gum even into the early morning hours in some of the city's most dangerous neighborhoods.

The streets and the seamy docks also teemed with youthful flower peddlers, fishmongers, and fruit sellers. Hogan reported that children as young as seven worked in the fish canneries and ten-year-old girls were common in local pickle factories. Other children clerked in stores or drove delivery wagons. When work failed to bring in acceptable funds, some boys followed drunks begging for coins and looking for a chance to rob their mark if he passed out on the street.

Whether in a large city like San Francisco or in a small Kansas farming town, cats reproduced at alarming rates and created money-making possibilities for kids. While a large feline population helped control rodents, dozens of cats created an after dark nightmare because of all the noise they made on their nightly sojourns. Their trilling, hissing, caterwauling, screeching and howling kept folks awake at night. The problem was so bad that insomniacs would throw all sorts of objects—bootjacks, hair brushes, shoes, etc.—out the window to scare them off.

Town boys from Iowa to Utah decided to profit from these nightly feline frolics. After dark these mischievous lads would hide and howl like cats, enticing folks to toss things their way. The boys would then collect the items to sell the next day. When an 1885 article appeared in a Salt Lake City newspaper about an Iowa boy doing just that, a reader responded, "that is an old scheme."

The reader explained, "I tried the same thing when I was a boy and carried it on for two or three weeks. But one night, after making the air ring and shriek with my imitations, I concluded to give up the business. I was doing tolerably well for a boy, but all of a sudden, I decided to quit, and quit, I did.... The very last thing I gathered in was a load of birdshot from a double-barreled shotgun."

Even innocent mischief could be dangerous on the frontier, but work was serious business that could mean the difference between whether or not a child and possibly his or her family could eat that day, especially for indigent families.

Just as today, some families then were better off than others. Growing up in Abilene, Kansas, young David enjoyed a comfortable childhood. Though Abilene was long past its glory days as a wild and wooly cowtown, he loved to hear old-timers tell of the cattle-herding days. Their stories spawned in him a lifetime fascination with Western novels and a commitment to hard work to match their exploits. He and his six brothers not only did chores around their parents' property but also worked a small piece of land their father allotted each son to raise his own garden.

David recalled, "Each was privileged to raise any kind of vegetable he chose and to sell them, if possible, to the neighbors for a profit.... For my plot, I chose to grow sweet corn and cucumbers. I had made inquiries and decided that these were the most popular vegetables." With the profits he made one summer, he bought a baseball mitt. The work ethic his parents instilled in him, and the self-reliance he learned as a result served him well at the U.S. Military Academy, where he went by Dwight, his first name.

Dwight David Eisenhower went on to lead the successful Allied invasion into Normandy on D-Day and to become the thirty-fourth President of the United States. Though the family's survival did not depend on the tasks that he and his brothers accomplished, the chores he handled—either for his family's or his personal benefit—created a work ethic that served him and the nation well in adulthood.

Whether frontier children grew up in town or on the farm, the work they accomplished helped them develop confidence in themselves and a self-reliance to face unforeseen challenges for themselves, for their families and for their country as they entered the twentieth century.

Chapter Eight

# Making Ends Meet

When his father Isaac died, young Billy, at the age of eleven, discussed with his older sister "what he must do to help take care of Mother and the three sisters and little brother." After that meeting, Billy took his first job to support his family and make ends meet on their Kansas homestead.

Hired by a local freight company, he drove an oxen team and hauled hay for fifty cents a day to nearby Fort Leavenworth. Like many frontier children, dire economic circumstances forced him to take on various jobs outside the home to bring in a few dollars and cents. Next, he delivered messages three miles between the shipping office and the nearest telegraph bureau. By the time he was sixteen, Billy had herded oxen, scouted for the United States Army, fought Indians, prospected for gold during the Pike's Peak Rush, hunted buffalo and rode for the Pony Express.

Like Billy, many other boys and girls took on work outside the home or assumed farm and household duties so their parents could take paying jobs elsewhere to support the family. Billy, or William Frederick Cody as his folks christened him, was unlike the others, though. Later in life, Buffalo Bill, as he became known globally, parlayed those and subsequent frontier experiences into acts for his Wild West shows which carried the thrills—often exaggerated—of Old West life around the world. His subsequent skill as a frontier showman and publicity hound made him famous internationally and brought him wealth far beyond even his wildest childhood dreams.

Few of his youthful contemporaries ever achieved such fame or riches. They were too intent on surviving the moment and helping their families endure. Such was life on the frontier. Older boys often hired out to do farm chores for their neighbors while their maturing sisters took jobs in hotels, restaurants, and laundries or as housekeepers for more affluent folks.

Without those outside jobs, some families would have suffered because crops failed and money ran out. When that happened, hunger followed. In frontier west Texas, William Holden's clan suffered a year when drought withered their crops. Young William, who years later would become a west Texas historian, said his family "had to do everything on earth to keep alive." Their diet consisted of rabbits and "milk-less gravy." During hard times in Oklahoma, youngster Dollie Jones learned from her parents to drink enough water to fill her belly when their limited corncakes failed to satisfy her hunger. So bare was their cupboard, Dollie remembered having only a single piece of salt pork to grease the griddle for what little food they had to cook.

Texan Edna Matthews looked back at lean times when the eight-year-old and her family survived on a bluish milk, cornbread, and bacon so rancid it made her gag when she smelled it from thirty yards away. She was so hungry that at a subsequent wedding reception hosted by a more prosperous couple, she burst into tears when she was told she could eat her fill. "Everybody understood," she said years later.

Like William F. Cody, young plains pioneer Catherine Porter watched her father die, forcing her brother to work for a neighboring farmer. The grain and meat he received in payment helped the Porter family survive the loss. Hattie Lee and two of her brothers took jobs to assist her clan, the boys herding animals while she worked a series of occupations as cook, maid, and waitress. "When a child is out in the world … no one knows what a hard time she has."

In 1870 E.L. Brounson, a south Texas youth, had to find work. "My father was wounded in the Civil War and became an invalid," Brounson recalled, "so when I was twelve years old I went to work on the range to help support our family. I helped to clear the first pasture that was fenced in our part of the country."

After an accident blinded her mother, Silver City, New Mexico, lass Mamie Rose not only took on the housework but also all of the cooking for a household of fifteen. She was just eight years old at the time. After a decade of preparing meals for her kinfolks, she started fixing food for others, beginning a successful career as a caterer.

Even when children like Mamie left home to start their own lives, they sometimes sent money back to support their parents. One first-year Kansas teacher shared forty-five dollars of her hundred-and-twenty-five-dollar annual salary with her father to help him purchase horses. The next year, the educator surrendered a third of her hundred-and-eighty-dollar salary to assist him in buying a new wagon.

In the 1850s near the community of Easton in northeastern Kansas near where William Cody freighted hay to Fort Leavenworth, young Annie Gilkeson realized her father was a poor farmer unable to support his family on their homestead, despite his good intentions. As Annie explained it, "We soon found, however, that the business of farming was of secondary importance compared to the form of work which we were compelled to engage in—compelled is the right word. With no thought or intention of keeping an inn, we were obliged to do so."

During that decade, as westward migration exploded, the Gilkeson homestead stood near the road traveled by hundreds of passing settlers. The Gilkeson place was a convenient stopping point just a day's ride from Leavenworth. Annie remembered the travelers "just settled down on us like the hordes of hungry grasshoppers which came later." Annie believed her mother worked herself to death in accommodating the travelers and supplementing the income of their failing farm.

"She worked day and night to care for and feed these hungry people. I, then a child of eleven years, was her only assistance, as no other help could be obtained for love. One day, my mother went to town, leaving me in charge of the place. She expected to be away only during the noonday meal and thought I could put off anyone who might chance to come."

With the house quiet and no settlers approaching, Annie took her two younger sisters out to gather wild strawberries, which grew in abundance around their land. While picking berries, she heard someone speak to her. "Looking up, I saw a man. He said that he wanted something to eat; [and] also, that at the house there were a number of others in the same condition. I told him my mother was away, and that I could not serve them."

The visitor insisted Annie provide grub for them. Intimidated by the adult and his demands, she led her sisters back to the house and did the best she could from having watched her mother prepare meals. "I gathered up all I could find to eat in the house and set it before them. I made for them, I remember, my first coffee. With much misgiving, in regard to its quality, I served it to them. But they all praised it, said it was fine. Never in all my life did I get up a meal which received more praise and I felt more pride in."

On the opposite side of Kansas, fourteen-year-old John Norton and his siblings gathered bleached buffalo bones, which were sold for industrial uses back east. Factories pulverized the skeletons to produce fertilizer, bone china, buttons, and corset or buttonhooks. In 1878 Norton wrote in his diary, "We have sold some bones once and have started to get some more … Pa, Curt and I took the bones to town today. We had 1,710 pounds, a big load."

When Charley O'Kieffe's family in the Nebraska Sandhills learned a buyer was offering nine dollars a ton for "any kind of bones: buffalo, steer, wolf, even human bones," the entire clan gathered skeleton pieces in their wagon for a major payday. "There were so many bones on the prairie," one Kansas girl recalled, "the children easily gathered wagonloads," bringing in additional revenue while freeing their parents for other tasks.

Youngster John Norton also hunted rabbits to sell for meat and hides. South of Taos in New Mexico Territory, young Lorin Brown and a trio of friends laid out traps in adjacent streams to catch varmints for their hides. Each Saturday, they gathered their kill, skinned the animals, fleshed the pelts and stretched them to dry. When the animal skins were ready, they shipped them to Denver, where a fur and pelt house used them for various products.

In southern North Dakota, the Martin family was so poor in money and livestock that fourteen-year-old Lena and eleven-year-old John Martin actually worked on their farm as draft animals. They pulled a cart to haul stones for the foundation of a shed on their homestead. An equally indigent neighbor offered to buy the brother and sister each a pair of shoes for the approaching winter months if he could use them to pull his thresher after the harvest. Without their mother's permission, their dad agreed to indenture Lena and John to the neighbor despite the horrible task and living conditions at the nearby homestead. When she learned of the agreement, their mother scolded her husband for the arrangement and ordered him to get them back, shoes or no shoes. The next Sunday, when their neighbors were at church, their father kidnapped his own son and daughter and returned them home.

In one of the saddest stories of frontier desperation, a widowed father took a daughter to a grocery store in Medicine Bow, Wyoming, and approached the husband and wife proprietors with a proposition to help feed his family. "I'll trade you this girl for a sack of flour." The indigent dad then explained, "My wife died and left me with seven." When the store owners realized his offer was sincere, they accepted the trade for fear the girl might be otherwise left with less reputable guardians. A witness to the trade said, "The girl … stood with her hand shading her eyes, and watched him out of sight. She did not cry, and she never uttered a word."

Such was the pressure of making ends meet, especially after losing a parent, that this unnamed father was willing to exchange one of his seven kids for food to feed the others.

Western plains youngster George MacGinitie remembered he "earned my first man's wages at the age of ten," hiring on with a relative to drive a team of horses. DeWitt Clinton Grinnell, the baby in a family of seven children, started a diary at thirteen and chronicled his chores. He worked with his father in the field, chopped firewood, tended the garden, and even helped his mother with housework on occasion. Additionally, he often hired out to neighbors, listing chores such as "I drove Mr. Everetts cow for him. He gave me twenty-five cents for doing it … I have been down to Mr. Tynes helping sieve wheat today." Even though the pay was small, he turned over most of it to his parents, saving only a pittance for his own needs.

Kansas girl Olive Capper hired out to neighbors, especially during the late summer and fall, to help can and preserve the garden produce for the winter months. For payment, she received jars of the canned fruits and vegetables, helping put food on the family table.

While children often worked away from home, so did their parents, who left the youngsters in charge of the farm or ranch. As their father could make more money as a harness maker in a nearby town, thirteen-year-old Arthur Adams and his brother operated the homestead, "feeling the weight of that responsibility," remembered one of their kinfolks.

While their father and oldest brother left Kansas to deliver freight to Colorado mining camps, thirteen-year-old Joshua Wheatcraft and his sixteen-year-old brother managed their homestead. In their dad's absence, the two boys broke thirty-six acres of sod and sowed the land with cane for use as animal fodder. Having handled a myriad of chores from the time he was four, Gregory Lacey at sixteen managed the farm of his father, freeing his elder to bring in additional income from other sources.

On the south plains of Texas, the drought of 1893 devastated the Dyer family crops, the clan's entire corn production totaling a bushel and a half. "There's where we liked to starved to death," remembered son M.E. Dyer. He and his siblings scoured the stream beds for river grass, which they stripped of its seeds and sold for two dollars a bushel. That seed money plus the cash their father earned chopping and selling firewood got them through the tough times.

Losing a parent is always emotionally traumatic for children, but on the frontier it could be economically devastating as well. After her mother's death, Mary Olive Gray of Silverton, Colorado, handled all the cooking for herself and her father. Not knowing how to make biscuits, the ten-year-old had to write her grandmother for the recipe and instructions.

After losing his father, thirteen-year-old Texas panhandle resident R.T. Alexander assumed the role of provider for his widowed mother and his four younger siblings until his mother's ranch turned a profit. The youth cut wild hay along the Washita River bottom and freighted it thirty-five miles away to Mobeetie for sale. With the help of his siblings, he gathered buffalo bones, which brought eight dollars a ton in the town of Canadian, and made additional cash by selling wild turkeys he had shot. Until he was sixteen, he put meat on the family table by hunting deer, rabbits, and prairie chickens. When R.T. left home, he became a successful freighter.

At the age of eight, pintsized Mose Drachman quit school in Tucson to help his fatherless family of eleven survive. He had his most success walking the dusty streets of Tucson and shouting out advertisements for upcoming auctions. His success in drawing crowds and his savvy in observing the business side of the sales provided him a successful apprenticeship for a prosperous Arizona mercantile career.

After the Civil War, young teen Hiram Craig in Washington County, Texas, lost both his mother and father, making orphans of him, his six brothers and two sisters. Craig said, "This left the family in the hands of my oldest brother, who faithfully and conscientiously administered to our wants until we were able to take care of ourselves."

During the gold boom in Goldfield, Nevada, at the turn of the twentieth century, fifteen-year-old Joseph McDonald peddled newspapers and even took it on the chin, fighting in exhibition boxing matches to bring in money to provide for himself and his mother.

As a self-described "little stringy-head country girl" from Grayson County, Texas, Bennie Hughes started peddling fruit at nine years, selling peaches and other fruits on the courthouse square. "I kept saving my nickels and dimes, and every time I got enough to buy a dogie, I bought because it took dogies to make cows. I just kept this up until I got a start [in the cattle business] … I kept adding to my herd, riding the range, and cutting cattle until I had a nice business. When I was seventeen years old, I bought and sold cattle like a man."

Young Sarah Harkey was the fifth of thirteen children born in the 1850s and 1860s in San Saba County in central Texas. Her mother died giving birth to the family's last child. Three weeks later, her father passed away as well, orphaning thirteen siblings between the ages of seventeen and one month old. The brothers and sisters faced life on their own, save for the advice of an aunt and uncle who came for the funerals but lived too far away to stay or to assist them. The aunt took the newborn until he was old enough to return, then left the twelve other children to fend for themselves.

Of her parents' deaths, Sarah remembered, "I had not yet shed a tear. It seemed that all was in a gloom and a hard pressure upon my breast. My two older brothers and my two older sisters were weeping bitterly at intervals, but the weight upon my breast remained solid and firm. Thus, the days passed in gloom."

Gloomy or not, the siblings went about life, the boys working the farm and the sisters keeping the house, cooking, and helping their brothers as needed. With a bit of luck, they all survived a Comanche raid on their place, though the Indians stole Sarah's pony. "After the Indians made their raid and drifted west with all the horses they could get, and the scare of the people became cold, the boys went back and forth to cultivate the crop. This was so inconvenient and dangerous," Sarah recalled.

When the Harkey baby reached seven months old, the aunt returned him to his siblings, and the thirteen scratched out a living as best they could by themselves. Save for the Indian scare, their first year on their own was good, as crops were in the field and provisions stored for winter. But after the second year, the burden became more difficult. Friction and jealousies developed among the siblings because of the stresses of managing everything on their own.

Sarah described the situation years later. "No crops were raised at all, planting only for the stock to destroy and never taking heed to the repairing of fences, but still we had everything we needed. We were living off of what we had and nothing coming in, of which I never thought of. My great heart pressure had begun to soften. I could meditate over the loss of my parents and see the children scattering from home, which was against Father's will. I could now relieve my heartaches by the shedding of tears. I had begun to look into the future for more pleasant and happy days, when, lo, my oldest brother began to stay away from home. He was compelled to leave us and work to support us. All those lonely days, we would pass off the time as best we could."

Her oldest brother joined the Texas Rangers and sent home what money he could. Another brother split rails to buy food. The family survived, but not without missing some meals and worrying until every child left home to make his or her way in life.

In contrast to the Harkey family, John Taylor Waldorf, from the age of three until he was almost sixteen, lived in Virginia City, Nevada, on the Comstock Lode between 1873 and 1886. As the son of modestly successful parents, he never had to worry about having food on the table. He did have to hustle, however, to earn money for activities his parents might not have approved. So, he and his friends collected odds and ends to sell to a junk vendor.

"It was a poor day when we failed to gather something in the way of junk," Waldorf recalled. "We accumulated bits of wrought iron, cast iron, lead, zinc, copper, brass, and glass. We saved up coal-oil cans, sacks, and rags. Our mothers had all they could do to keep us from stripping the house of extra clothing.

Rags were quoted at half a cent a pound and … found us looking upon everything in the cloth line as rags."

Waldorf and his pals succeeded because of Virginia City's sole junkman, a fellow named Robinson, who carried "so many dimes and quarters and halves in a dirty leather sack." Robinson had a "yard piled high with junk" and a genius for arithmetic. The local boys considered Robinson's financial standing second only to Comstock mining magnates John W. Mackay and James G. Fair.

"Money from that dirty leather sack was responsible for much enthusiasm and more noise," Waldorf remembered. "The money (allowance) that came from home always had a string to it. We were expected to spend it like little gentlemen. What we got from Robinson's, we scattered around in a way that would bring the most joy to our heathen souls."

Besides foraging for junk, Waldorf and his friends also scrounged for tickets to various performances at Virginia City's Piper Opera House, as the stage added additional joys to their frugal lives. As a result, they came to admire the silver king John W. Mackay, who had a generous streak in him, unlike his mining rival James G. Fair. Mackay often passed out bills and coins to the young boys that played around the mines.

On nights when Mackay attended the opera house, forty or fifty penniless boys congregated by the theater, "hoping for miracles as they stood outside the entrance," Waldorf recalled. John Piper, the opera house owner, "would sit in the box office and scowl at us until his fat face was all wrinkles."

"Then Mackay would come along, nod his head toward the gang, and say, 'John, how much for the bunch?' A heavenly smile would wreath John's face as he counted us and announced the result. At fifty cents a head, it generally came to about twenty dollars. Mackay would say, 'Let the kids see the show,' and John [Piper] would deal out our tickets with one hand while he gathered in the twenty with the other."

Reflecting on the generosity years later, Waldorf said, "We would enjoy the show, and what is more we would think better of all mankind because John Mackay had remembered that he was once a boy and had given us something from his great store.... When he died, we children of the Comstock, although most of us had not seen him for years, felt that we had lost a near and dear friend."

Few frontier children had it as good as young Waldorf with his millionaire benefactor on the Comstock Lode. Those less fortunate ones often had to take jobs to help the family or support themselves. In one instance, a widower remarried, and his new wife cared little for his children and sent one son out on his own at fourteen years of age.

Other children offered their services to the public through newspaper ads or answered advertisements from families needing help. In an 1895 *St. Louis Post-Dispatch* ad one boy sought employment as "Boy of 13 wishes work; cash boy, chore boy or any kind of employment." In 1897 the *Deseret News* in Salt Lake City ran ads of children seeking work, including "Girl for general housework. No Washing" and "Boy 16 years, will do chores, look after horse or cow as part payment for board during winter."

People also advertised for pintsized employees. In an 1879 want ad in the *Nebraska City News Press*, W. Hawke sought "A good boy (German preferred) to do chores etc." An 1887 "Wanted—Help" advertisement by Martin & Company in the *Los Angeles Times* sought, among others, "Boy To Herd, $10 a month, room and board; … boy to chore in place, $10 a month, room and board; … boy in a private place, $15, room and board; … 75 waiter girls, $6 to $8 a week; … 5 nurse girls, $15 to $20 a month …." Stated an 1889 ad in the *Salt Lake Herald*, "Wanted: A Boy About Twelve years old to do chores on a ranch." The 1895 *Independent-Record* in Helena, Montana, ran ads for the Helena Employment Agency seeking "Second girl for family in city, $20 … Girl for ranch, $30 … One girl for family of four in city, $25 … Girl on ranch at Lavina, $20."

Frontier youngsters, like their parents, learned to make do if that was what it took to make ends meet. They would take jobs far beyond their years. Vagabonds such as young William F. Cody, long before he became known as "Buffalo Bill," bounced from job to job. One of his earliest experiences was with the Pony Express, helping the company build several way stations for riders to exchange horses. Later he worked as a rider, carrying mail on segments of the nineteen-hundred-mile route.

By a popular legend, the Pony Express posted an early help-wanted ad for "Young, skinny, wiry fellows not over eighteen. Must be expert riders, willing to risk death daily. Orphans preferred." Though that ad appears to have been manufactured long after the demise of the mail service, it captured the glamor that would later be associated with the temporary delivery service. Like many western occupations, the glamor came more from nostalgia than reality.

The Pony Express maintained a policy of hiring no riders under sixteen years old, but the company had no way of checking or confirming the age of applicants beyond their stated word. Thus, some younger boys rode for the outfit. One was Billy Tate, who covered a section of the Pony Express route near Ruby Valley, Nevada. During an 1860 Indian uprising, a band of Paiutes attacked the young rider, chasing him into rocks where he killed seven of his attackers before being riddled with arrows. To acknowledge his bravery, Tate's assailants neither scalped him nor mutilated his body.

Whether Tate entered the express service to find adventure, to help his folks, or to just make ends meet remains unknown. What is known is that Tate was only fourteen when he died.

The story of the Childers brothers sums up the work history of their frontier peers, both boys and girls. When their father left their modest Texas ranch to manage a larger spread in another county for additional income, his sons W.H. and Cyrus Childers took on major responsibilities. Recalled W.H., "Dad put me and my younger bud, Cyrus, in charge of the place and with orders not to neglect it but to work it like it belonged to us. And, that we done. Cy and me sure run that place, even though he wasn't but nine and I was thirteen when Dad left."

Both brothers performed so well managing their "stock farm," as W.H. called it, that when he turned eighteen, his father put him to work on the ranch he managed. W.H. hired on as a cowboy "at twenty dollars a month with chuck." Cyrus later joined him.

As W.H. explained it, "That was the way of the old-timer days, though. Kids got to be men a heap quicker than they do nowadays, and Cy and me went to the roundups just like we were men."

Chapter Nine

# Pintsized Lessons

Pintsized frontier boys and girls did indeed grow up faster than American children in subsequent generations.

As an adult, the Canadian-born American journalist whose columns and musings earned him the title of "the poet laureate of common sense," Walt Mason offered tongue-in-cheek reflections on frontier childhood. He mused:

> I'd like to be a boy again without a woe or care, with freckles scattered on my face and hayseed in my hair; I'd like to rise at four o'clock and do a hundred chores, and saw the wood and feed the hogs and lock the stable doors; and herd the hens and watch the bees and take the mules to drink, and teach the turkeys how to swim so that they wouldn't sink; and milk about a hundred cows and bring in wood to burn, and stand out

> in the sun all day and churn and churn and churn; and wear my brother's cast-off clothes and walk four miles to school, and get a licking every day for breaking some old rule; and go home at night and do the chores once more, and milk the cows and feed the hogs and curry mules galore; and then crawl wearily upstairs to seek my little bed, and hear dad say, "That worthless boy! He doesn't earn his bread!" I'd like to be a boy again, a boy has so much fun; his life is just a round of mirth, from rise to set of sun; I guess there's nothing pleasanter than closing stable doors, and herding hens, and chasing bees and doing evening chores.

Mason could just as easily have written a similar piece on young frontier girls, though he would have had to list additional tasks such as cooking, housekeeping, sewing, washing, managing a household, and raising younger siblings. By necessity, daughters more often ventured into the realm of their father's chores than their brothers did into their mother's work around the house.

This bias was represented when a Chicago reporter accompanied an Iowa farm couple to the city's Englewood orphanage on Sixty-sixth Street in search of a child to adopt. The farmer told the nursery attendant, "My wife wants a girl baby with blue eyes. She ain't particular about the hair being dark or light, but she don't want no bald heads."

The accompanying staff member noted girls were hard to come by in the orphanage because "everybody knows how much more docile, lovable, and desirable generally girls are than boys, and they are snapped up accordingly." On this day, only a one baby girl was available for adoption.

"Don't you be so foolish as to take a girl," the orphanage attendant said. "Girls ain't no use on a farm. What you want is a good, healthy boy, who will soon lend a helping hand to the chores."

"I don't know," replied the farmer. "You can make a boy out of a girl, so to speak, for she can help in the chores if need be, but you can't make a girl out of a boy. They won't do housework, no how."

The newspaper article neglected to report the farm couple's choice, but the account demonstrates how girls handled a wider variety of chores than did their brothers around the farm and ranch. However, as daughters matured, they were often pushed into more traditional roles of housekeeping and child rearing.

Some female teenagers like Ada Vroomaan rebelled and went out on their own. Living in the Cherokee Strip, Ada tired of tending the house and her younger brother. When she discovered she could teach school once she passed a qualifying test and found a place to hold classes, she did both. Ada entered teaching and earned her own keep at the age of sixteen. On the frontier, young girls commonly became school mistresses as early as fifteen, fourteen, and even thirteen years of age, barely older than some of their students.

Two months before she turned sixteen, Laura Ingalls accepted an 1882 South Dakota teaching position to help her family make ends meet. Over the next two years, she not only taught three terms of school but also worked for the local dressmaker to bring in extra money. That work ethic ultimately helped her become a nationally known author, beloved to this day for her frontier stories.

Just as girls routinely handled more varied chores than boys, children also managed a greater variety of tasks than their parents. By the time they became adults, men and women tended to handle jobs typically associated with their gender, unless separation or death of one forced a change. Sons and daughters, however, did whatever they were instructed to do. Simply put, pintsized pioneers became the most adaptable workforce on the frontier. They assumed many responsibilities far beyond their years. In the process, they carried workloads that helped their families survive.

Further, they gained characteristics that would help them succeed later in life. By the turn of the twentieth century, some newspapers were reporting the long-term value of childhood labor. Idaho's *Bonners Ferry Herald* in 1898 reported "eighty percent of the men in the United States now worth one hundred thousand dollars and more have risen from the laboring classes." While the paper admitted "this floating statement can hardly be verified by exact figures," it noted "it is likely to be quite within the bounds of truth." The reason for their financial success, the paper argued, was that "the foundations of their fortunes were laid in small earnings, small savings, small spendings." The laboring class understood that truth better than the idle class.

During the same decade, the *Abilene* (Texas) *Reporter* encouraged youngsters to "Work, Boys, Work!" The newspaper reported, "The boys of this town who are doing absolutely nothing would improve their opportunities in life if they would get some honorable employment ... your worth will be recognized and you will someday be rewarded with a good position, or if not will be fitted by your experience to enter into business for yourselves ... you will find yourself on the road to prosperity and happiness, while the loafers will be very fortunate to keep out of the poor house, or from living off of their good old parents, or out of the prison. Work, Boys, Work!"

The works of author Horatio Alger, Jr., between 1868 and 1899, imbedded the rags-to-riches narrative in the national culture. Alger penned young adult novels about poverty-stricken youths whose hard and honest labor propelled them up into the middle class or higher. His early books focused on urban kids and their successes. His poor-boy-makes-good theme remained consistent throughout his own successful career, but by the late 1870s he had broadened his stories to use settings from the American West.

Gainful work by boys and girls, whether by necessity or by choice, came to represent in the popular media of the day a brighter future for the individual and for the country. Out West childhood labor was essential for the present because the West would never have been civilized without it.

Historian Elliott West, an authority on children in the Old West, said, "They played an indispensable part in western settlement." He added, "They helped create a modern region and boost the nation toward power and affluence. Until their accomplishments are recognized, we cannot begin to understand the economic and human dimensions of western history."

That necessity-induced infringement on childhood, though, concerned some Victorian era observers like English explorer and writer Isabella A. Bird, who traversed the Rocky Mountains and its mining culture in 1873. She was appalled at what she saw. "One of the most painful things in the Western States and territories," she wrote, "is the extinction of childhood. I have never seen any children, only debased imitations of men and women, cankered by greed and selfishness, and asserting and gaining complete independence of their parents at ten years old. The atmosphere in which they are brought up is one of greed, godlessness and frequently of profanity. Consequently, these sweet things seem like flowers in the desert. Except for love, which here as everywhere raises life into the ideal, this is a wretched existence."

Evaluating the impact of the frontier household on children, historian West more than a century later offered a softer view. "The companionate family was alive and healthy on the frontier, and most parents treated their young with concern and an awareness of their emotional needs. Mothers especially gave them affection and close attention during infancy and early childhood, those first two years of life most crucial to their emotional security. Children also made lives for themselves away from their families, cultivating close friendships with others their ages and making their surroundings into playgrounds."

As an adult, Sallie Reynolds Matthews offered her perspective of growing up on the west Texas frontier. "In thinking of these bygone days, how we were struggling and bending every effort for the benefit of our children's education and culture, trying to furnish them privileges that we in our pioneer upbringing had been denied, I am reminded of something my dear old mother, sitting quietly by, observing with her keen mind all that was going on, said to me one day. 'Sallie, if your children are not a whole lot better and a whole lot smarter than you are, there is lots of time and money wasted on them.'"

Without a doubt, times remained challenging on the frontier, but the children adapted not just to their chores but to their situations. They made work into games where they could, and often observed their environment in ways their elders never did. Frontier girls on the prairies had fond memories in later years of the spring flowers that created a colorful palette across the landscape. Young boys exulted in the freedom to explore the countryside when they finished their tasks. Some youngsters, male and female, kept journals of the plant life they found or the wildlife they encountered, describing flora and fauna like junior scientists. Their environment was a world to investigate, even when their parents viewed it as a land to tame and profit from, even if that benefit was merely to feed their family.

Historian West continued, "A typical adult pioneer, to be sure, was an optimist inspired by dreams of gain. Yet pioneers did more than transform the country, and certainly they worried about more than making profits. They went west, also determined to build what they considered a proper social order. The focus of that was not the field and the mine but the family, the home, and the children."

This book has focused on the chores the pintsized pioneers did and what it cost them in time, freedom and worry as they grew into adults. However, the lessons they learned accomplishing so many tasks as children served them well as they matured. First, they gained essential skills and knowledge about the basics of life so they could better adapt to its challenges. They understood where the food and the fiber came from to fill their bellies and to clothe their backs. Additionally, they realized success is irrigated by the sweat of their own brows.

Second, they gained confidence and a sense of worth from every successful task. Even when they failed at an assignment, they learned valuable lessons for future improvement. Confidence spawned self-esteem and pride in the accomplishments.

Third, young boys and girls became self-reliant. When mother and father were too overworked to help, the youngsters figured out ways to handle their duties. As the childhood historian West explained it, "At an early age, far earlier than most youngsters today, frontier children were expected to deal with the demands and pressures of adulthood. They were given heavy responsibilities and exhausting work in some of the most difficult environments the country could offer. Many were expected to make important, even vital decisions."

Fourth, they learned the value of cooperation and teamwork. Many times it took the entire household to make ends meet, especially after the loss of a parent. Each family member past infancy played a role in the clan's survival as even the slightest chore by the littlest child freed up older siblings and parents to attend to more pressing needs.

Fifth, hard times tempered children with the understanding that difficulties do not last forever. Weathering the challenges prepared youngsters for future trials as adults, both in their family and professional lives.

Finally, the work provided adolescents a sense of self-satisfaction in accomplishing a task that might have been intimidating until attempted and completed. The frontier fashioned youngsters for success and instilled in them a work ethic whether they wanted it or not. William F. "Buffalo Bill" Cody, Dwight David Eisenhower, and Laura Ingalls are examples of the frontier work ethic and its reach into the future.

Forced from home to help support his family after his father's death, Cody handled a myriad of jobs. Those experiences provided grist for many of the acts that he would employ in 1883 when he founded his traveling show Buffalo Bill's Wild West. For years he journeyed across America and later Europe, reenacting in circus-like performances many of the thrilling adventures that elevated the frontier into legend. Because of his flamboyance and his world-wide exposure, by the end of the nineteenth century, Buffalo Bill was thought to be the most famous man on earth.

Far less flamboyant than Buffalo Bill, but even more important for the future of the world was Dwight D. Eisenhower, who came from a more privileged background than Cody. Even so, his parents instilled in him a strong work ethic, an overwhelming sense of responsibility, and a sense of teamwork as one of seven brothers. Those values served both him and humanity admirably during World War II, when he commanded the successful Allied invasion of Normandy in the most complex military operation in history. Eisenhower would go on to serve two terms as president in one of the most consequential American administrations of the twentieth century.

Fifty years after Laura Ingalls took her initial teaching job in South Dakota, she published her first book *Little House in the Big Woods* under her married name, Laura Ingalls Wilder. The book recalled the trials and triumphs of frontier life. That and her subsequent books, including *Little House on the Prairie*, would make her one of the nation's most beloved authors, especially among young girls. The lessons of work, thrift, and family she extolled in books were the same values that she learned as a child. Those adolescent teachings helped her succeed as an author.

Cody, Eisenhower, and Wilder are but three examples of the success of pintsized pioneers in later life. The standards instilled in them and their frontier generation served them and the nation well.

Frontier childhood historian Elliott West explained that ethic and its contemporary relevance this way: "A child's life in the developing West encouraged traits especially useful in the contemporary world. Among these were a resilient strength, a self-reliance and sense of worth, and a tested understanding that hard times can be endured. Most children must have taken into their adult lives a faith in the family and its ability to adjust to trying circumstances. In the particulars of pioneer childhood were grounded qualities commonly associated with the modern West, among them an openness toward strangers, a confidence in dealing with fresh challenges, a kinship with what remains of the natural setting, and a pride—albeit an often grudging pride—in its contrariness."

Just as eloquently, a Kansas pioneer mother named Margaret Marshall—years before Dr. West began his childhood research—summed up the importance of family and children in settling the West. "When all is said and done, man alone never settled a country, never built an empire, never even stayed 'put' unless accompanied by wife and children.... The unconquerable spirit of man may subdue, but it never yet has settled a new country; the family does that."

Children may not have won the West, but they tamed it, one chore at a time. In the end, the character those tasks instilled in them not only served them well as children but also as adults heading into the challenges of the twentieth century. They believed they could do anything.

Acknowledgements

This book was written for young adults to show them the contributions of their adolescent forebears in settling the American West and in making the nation the greatest on earth. Further, it demonstrates the value of children's work not only in building the United States but also in developing the character that served them well in their adult lives.

We would like to think that we are pioneers in examining the role of adolescents on the frontier. We are not. Though we may have been among the first to address the topic for a young adult audience, we relied on the published works of the true pioneers in the field.

First among them is Elliott West. *His Growing Up with the Country: Childhood on the Far Western Frontier* was the seminal work in the field, providing an expansive look at the role of boys and girls in the American West. To our knowledge, his 1989 book was the first major publication by a professional historian on the topic and remains a pivotal work more than a third of a century later. As with all of Dr. West's books, it is insightful and written with a flair that demonstrates his talent as both a historian and a writer.

While Dr. West provided the most substantial treatment of pioneer children throughout the West, several others offered enlightening regional studies. These scholars and their works include Marilyn Irvin Holt, *Children of the Western Plains: The Nineteenth-Century Experience*; Linda Peavy and Ursula Smith, *Frontier Children*; Elizabeth Hampsten, *Settlers' Children: Growing Up on the Great Plains*; and Craig Miner, *West of Wichita: Settling the High Plains of Kansas, 1865-1890.* Multiple books by Cathy Luchetti were also helpful in this process.

The classic works of some early historians of the American West also offered valuable insights. These included *The Great Plains* by Walter Prescott Webb; *The Sod-House Frontier, 1854-1890* by Everett Dick; and *The Trail Drivers of Texas* by J. Marvin Hunter. Also helpful were *Son of the Old West: The Odyssey of Charlie Siringo: Cowboy, Detective, Writer of the Wild Frontier* by Nathan Ward and *Texas Cowboys: Memories of the Early Days,* edited by Jim Lanning and Judy Lanning.

Memoirs of several pioneers about their childhoods on the frontier were also helpful. Those reminiscences were written by John Taylor Waldorf, Edwin Lewis Bennett, Hamlin Garland, Frances Bramlette Farris, Sallie Reynolds Matthews, Lily Klasner, Agnes Morley Cleaveland, and Sarah Harkey Hall. All of these and other authors whose works were beneficial in the writing of this book are listed in the bibliography.

Over the years our love of the history of the Old West and our passion for writing about it have been supported by our membership and participation in Western Writers of America, as caring and supportive an organization as you will ever find devoted to writing. Some members stand out for their support in our efforts and their friendship. The late Jeanne Williams and Elmer Kelton, giants in the field of Western writing, served as writing mentors early in our careers. No writer has been more supportive later in our careers than Chris Enss, a talented author as demonstrated by her *New York Times* bestselling author credentials and the best we've ever seen at marketing books.

Two writing couples also deserve our sincere acknowledgement. Fellow Texas residents Mike and Beverly Cox have been longtime friends. We may not agree on everything, but we have fun and laughs even over our differences. Tom and Marilyn Clagett, our New Mexico neighbors, are a delightful and fun couple with great insights into writing and life. We enjoy our monthly phone conversations and the times we can get together in person.

This book would not have been possible without the fifty-year partnership of the co-authors. That relationship has not only produced books, but also a son and a daughter. Raising Scott and Melissa was the true joy of our young married lives. The addition of Celeste, our daughter-in-law, and John, our son-in-law, enhanced our family and our fun. The subsequent arrival of our grandchildren Hannah, Cora, Miriam,

Carys, and Jackson made our family complete. Through them all we have been truly blessed.

Working on this project together has truly been a blessing for us both. We hope that young readers of *Pintsized Pioneers* will find passages that speak to them and provide insights they can apply to their own lives.

*Preston Lewis*
*and*
*Harriet Kocher Lewis*
*San Angelo, Texas*
*July 4, 2024*

# Glossary

*Acequia:* Spanish term for an irrigation ditch or canal

*Appomattox:* Virginia site where General Robert E. Lee surrendered the Army of Northern Virginia to General Ulysses S. Grant to effectively end the American Civil War in April 1865

*Bovine:* n. an ox or cow; adj. of or relating to cattle

*Buffalo wallow:* a depression in flat prairie land that holds rain water and runoff; when dry used by buffalo to roll over on the ground and remove dead hair

*Capillary action:* the tendency of a liquid in a tube or absorbent material to rise or fall as a result of surface tension

*Centaur:* a mythological creature with the upper body of a human and the lower body and legs of a horse

*Churn:* n. a device or container in which butter is made by agitating milk or cream; v. to agitate or turn milk or cream into butter

*Cistern:* an underground reservoir to store rainwater or a tank for storing water

*Coal oil:* a flammable liquid obtained from the distillation of bituminous coal, often used for lamp illumination in the nineteenth century

*Dogie:* a ranch country term for a calf that has lost its mother, a bovine orphan, pronounced "doe-gee"
*Dugout:* a shelter dug in a hillside or in the ground and often roofed with sod
*Euphemism:* a mild word or expression substituted for a harsher term when referring to something unpleasant or embarrassing
*Gingham:* a lightweight, plain-woven cotton cloth, usually checked in white and another color
*Great Plains:* a North American expanse of flat prairie and grassland, extending from Canada south to Texas and bordered on the east by the 100th meridian and on the west by the Rocky Mountains
*Homestead Acts:* a series of federal laws after 1860 that allowed citizens to claim government land as their own, provided they met certain residential requirements
*Jowls:* the lower part of an animal's cheek, especially when it is fleshy or drooping
*Kerosene:* a flammable liquid distilled from petroleum and used for frontier illumination among other things
*Middlings:* bulk goods of medium grade, especially flour of medium fineness or a granular product from milling grain
*Milch Cow:* a cow producing milk or one kept for her milk
*Muslin:* a plain-woven cotton fabric
*Ollas:* Spanish for a type of pot or jar made from earthenware

*Placer:* a location where gold is found in the deposits of gravel, sand, clay, silt, and other materials eroded by running water, usually in a valley

*Rick:* a stack or pile of hay, grain, straw, or animal hides, particularly buffalo

*Rocker:* placer mining term for a hand-operated device used to agitate gravel and water to separate gold from worthless materials.

*Shoat:* a young pig just after weaning

*Sluice:* placer mining term for a series of wooden troughs or boxes lined with obstructions for washing out large quantities of gravel.

*Sod House/Soddy/Soddies:* a dwelling/dwellings made of sod or earthen blocks in regions where timber is scarce

*Staples:* a food consumed in such quantities that it is a major portion of a standard diet; staples include flour, sugar, coffee, etc.

*Straw:* dried stalks of grain, used especially as fodder or as material for thatching, packing, or weaving

*Swill:* kitchen refuse and scraps of waste food mixed with water for feeding to pigs.

*Switchback:* a zigzagging trail or road ascending steep hills or mountains

*Tallow:* a hard fatty substance made from rendered animal fat, used in making candles and soap

*Tick:* the fabric case of a pillow or mattress or a mattress consisting of tick and its filling.

*Tow Sack:* a large sack or bag traditionally made of burlap; also called a gunnysack

*Transcontinental Railroad:* a United States railroad built between 1863 and 1869 and connecting the existing eastern U.S. rail network at Council Bluffs, Iowa, with the Pacific coast at Oakland, California, on San Francisco Bay

*Treadle:* a swiveling or lever device pressed by the foot to power a device like a sewing machine

*Trundle bed:* a low bed that can be pushed under a higher bed when not in use

*Type:* a rectangular block of wood or metal bearing the relief character of a letter, number, or symbol used in early printing processes

*Waddie/Waddies:* temporary employee/employees who round out a ranch outfit during busy times

*Windlass:* a type of winch used to lower and hoist buckets from wells.

*Zion:* a metaphor for a unified society of Latter-Day Saints gathered together as members of the church

Bibliography

# For Further Reading

*A Kid on the Comstock: Reminiscences of a Virginia City Childhood* by John Taylor Waldorf (University of Nevada Press, Reno, 1970)

*A Lady's Life in the Rocky Mountains* by Isabella Bird (Digireads.com Publishing, 2019)

*A Pioneer Sampler: The Daily Life of a Pioneer Family in 1840* by Barbara Greenwood, illustrated by Heather Collins (Houghton Mifflin Co., Boston, 1994)

*Boom Town Boy in Old Creede Colorado* by Edwin Lewis Bennett and Agnes Wright Spring (Sage Books, Chicago, 1966)

*Boy Life on the Prairie* by Hamlin Garland (Bison Books, University of Nebraska Press, 1899 & 1961)

*Cat Tales of the Old West: Poems, Puns & Perspectives on Frontier Felines* by Preston Lewis (Bariso Press, San Angelo, Texas, 2021)

*Children of the West: Family Life on the Frontier* by Cathy Luchetti (W.W. Norton & Co., New York, 2001)

*Children of the Western Plains: The Nineteenth-Century Experience* by Marilyn Irvin Holt (Irvin R. Dee, Chicago, 2003)

*Everyday Life in the 1800s* by Marc McCutcheon (Writer's Digest Books, Cincinnati, 1992)

*From Rattlesnakes to Road Agents: Rough Times on the Frio* by Frances Bramlette Farris, edited by C.L. Sonnichsen (Texas Christian University Press, Fort Worth, 1985)

*Frontier Children* by Linda Peavy and Ursula Smith (University of Oklahoma Press, Norman, 1999)

*Glittering Misery: Dependents of the Indian Fighting Army* by Patricia Y. Stallard (University of Oklahoma Press, Norman, 1978)

*Gold in the Black Hills* by Watson Parker (University of Nebraska Press, Lincoln, 1966)

*Growing Up with the Country: Childhood on the Far Western Frontier* by Elliott West (University of New Mexico Press, Albuquerque, 1989)

*Home on the Range: A Culinary History of the American West* by Cathy Luchetti (W.W. Norton & Co., New York, 1993)

*Interwoven: A Pioneer Chronicle* by Sallie Reynolds Matthews (Texas A&M University Press, College Station, 1936, 1958 & 1982)

*I Walked to Zion: True Stories of Young Pioneers on the Mormon Trail* by Susan Arrington Madsen (Deseret Book Co., Salt Lake City, 1994)

*Letters by Lamplight: A Woman's View of Everyday Life in South Texas, 1873-1883* by Lois E. Myers (Baylor University Press, Waco, 1991)

*My Childhood Among Outlaws* by Lily Klasner, edited by Eve Ball (University of Arizona Press, Tucson, 1972)

*No Life for a Lady* by Agnes Morley Cleaveland (University of Nebraska Press, Lincoln, 1977)

*Nothing but Prairie and Sky: Life on the Dakota Range in the Early Days* by Walker D. Wyman (University of Oklahoma Press, Norman, 1954)

*Pioneer Children on the Journey West* by Emmy E. Werner (Westview Press, Boulder, Colorado, 1995)

*Pioneer Women: Voices from the Kansas Frontier* by Joanna L. Stratton (Simon and Schuster, New York, 1981)

*Red Blood and Black Ink: Journalism in the Old West* by David Dary (Alfred A. Knopf, New York, 1998)

*Settlers' Children: Growing Up on the Great Plains* by Elizabeth Hampsten (University of Oklahoma Press, Norman, 1991)

*Small Worlds: Children & Adolescents in America, 1850-1950,* by Elliott West and Paula Petrik, editors (University of Kansas Press, Lawrence, 1992)

*So Much to Be Done: Women Settlers on the Mining and Ranching Frontier* by Ruth B. Moynihan, Susan Armitage, and Christiane Fischer Dichamp, editors (University of Nebraska Press, Lincoln, 1990)

*Sod Busting: How Families Made Farms on the Nineteenth-Century Plains* by David B. Danbom (Johns Hopkins University Press, Baltimore, 2014)

*Son of the Old West: The Odyssey of Charlie Siringo: Cowboy, Detective, Writer of the Wild Frontier* by Nathan Ward (Atlantic Monthly Press, New York, 2023)

*Surviving on the Texas Frontier: The Journal of an Orphan Girl in San Saba County* by Sarah Harkey Hall (Eakin Press, Austin, 1996)

*Texas Cowboys: Memories of the Early Days* by Jim Lanning and Judy Lanning, editors (Texas A&M University Press, College Station, 1984)

*The Bonanza West: The Story of the Western Mining Rushes, 1848-1900* by William S. Greever (University of Oklahoma Press, Norman, 1963)

*"The Crucial Role of Prairie Coal,"* by Ralph A. Smith, *Celebrating 100 Years, West Texas Historical Review* (West Texas Historical Association, Lubbock, 2024)

*The Expansion of Everyday Life, 1860-1876* by Daniel E. Sutherland (University of Arkansas Press, Fayetteville, 2000)

*The Great Plains* by Walter Prescott Webb (Grosset & Dunlap, New York, 1931)

*The Quirt and the Spur: Vanishing Shadows of the Texas Frontier* by Edgar Rye (Texas Tech University Press, Lubbock, 2000)

*The Sod-House Frontier, 1854-1890,* by Everett Dick (University of Nebraska Press, Lincoln, 1937 & 1954)

*The Trail Drivers of Texas* by J. Marvin Hunter (University of Texas Press, Austin, 1985)
*West of Wichita: Settling the High Plains of Kansas, 1865-1890* by Craig Miner (University of Kansas Press, Lawrence, 1986)
*Women of the West* by Cathy Luchetti (W.W. Norton & Co., New York, 1982)

# About the Authors

Preston and Harriet Lewis have been a team for more than fifty years since they first met and married at Baylor University. Preston has earned multiple national awards for his fiction and nonfiction while Harriet is an award-winning editor with their Bariso Press.

A journalist by training, Preston has published more than fifty fiction and nonfiction works on the American West. Western Writers of America (WWA) has honored Lewis with two Spur Awards. The native Texan is the recipient of ten Will Rogers Medallion Awards, including six gold medallions for western humor, short stories, and traditional Westerns.

In 2021 he was inducted into the Texas Institute of Letters for his literary accomplishments. Preston is a past president of WWA and the West Texas Historical Association, which named him a fellow in 2016.

Harriet Kocher Lewis is editor and publisher of Bariso Press. Titles she has edited have been honored with Will Rogers Medallion Awards, Spur Finalist designations and Independent Author Awards.

A native Pennsylvanian, Harriet spent her professional career as a physical therapist, first in clinical settings and then in an academic environment. At Angelo State she taught medical documentation and wrote and edited numerous scientific papers as well as a chapter in a clinical education textbook. She is co-author with Preston of three books in the *Magic Machine Series* published by Bariso Press.

Harriet holds a bachelor's degree from Baylor University in biology and physical therapy and a master's degree from Texas Tech in kinesiology. Preston holds a bachelor's degree from Baylor and a master's degree from Ohio State University, both in journalism. He earned a second master's degree in history from Angelo State University.

They are parents of a son and a daughter and grandparents of four girls and a boy. They reside in San Angelo, Texas.

*E-mail*: barisopress@gmail.com
*Facebook*: prestonlewisauthor
*Website*: prestonlewisauthor.com

Printed in the USA
CPSIA information can be obtained
at www.ICGtesting.com
LVHW010107130724
785372LV00023B/113